JOEL CHANDLER HARRIS

PLANTATION STORYTELLER

JOEL CHANDLER HARRIS

JOEL CHANDLER HARRIS

(Uncle Remus)

PLANTATION STORYTELLER

By ALVIN F. HARLOW

ILLUSTRATED BY W. C. NIMS

JULIAN MESSNER, INC.

NEW YORK

PUBLISHED BY JULIAN MESSNER, INC.

8 WEST FORTIETH STREET, NEW YORK

EIGHTH PRINTING, 1957

MANUFACTURED IN THE UNITED STATES OF AMERICA

BY MONTAUK BOOKBINDING CORPORATION, NEW YORK

Contents

Foreword

"Lives of great men all remind us
We can make our lives—"

WELL, perhaps we can't just count on making
our lives "sublime," but certainly, since we are
not poets looking for rimes, we can make our
lives useful, or happy. Joel Chandler Harris was a great
man, and his life was both a happy and a useful one. His
life's work did not cease with his death, for he wrote books
in which we may find the secret of his happiness and use-
fulness and make it our own. When we read the books he
wrote and the books that have been written about him, we
find that there was nothing much out of the ordinary in
the circumstances of his life except the uses he made of
them.

Eatonton, in middle Georgia, where Joel was born, was
a small town, and dull, if you stopped to think about it.
Joel didn't find Eatonton dull, for he was a boy who liked
fun; so he sharpened his wits to find occasions for fun,
and he did well enough by himself without doing anyone
else any harm. It is true that he lacked what are called
"advantages," but the real advantages of boyhood are

health, a cheerful disposition, and kind friends. He had these in abundance.

His boyhood was not all play. His mother had to make a living for them both when he was little. As he grew older he realized that he must take care of his mother. When a chance for employment came, it seemed to him not only a duty but an opportunity.

Turnwold, where he went to learn the printer's trade, was a big place in the country nine miles from Eatonton. It might have seemed duller than Eatonton if Joel had stopped to think about it. But he was too busy learning the ways of the print shop, reading books which Mr. Turner, his employer, lent him from his own library, and finding out what was going on in every corner of the plantation.

Particularly he was interested in the Negroes. Mr. Turner owned many slaves, and since he treated them well, they dwelt contentedly in the "quarters." They had their work and their play; they lived their own lives, and kept up customs of their own. Some of the Negroes were great story tellers, and the stories they told were of animals who talked and acted like human beings. These tales were older than the black folks who related them, and had gathered the wisdom and humor of many generations of narrators. Joel didn't know it, but as he listened happily to this ancient African folklore, he was laying up stores of pleasure which some day he would pass on to other listeners far from the old plantation.

This is the way Joel Chandler Harris's life began, and it went on in much the same way. He never found the common things of life dull. He discovered a lively interest in the doings and sayings of ordinary people. On the plantation he had learned the printer's trade; he had learned to write verse and prose which Mr. Turner was glad to print in his little newspaper, *The Countryman*. When Joel left the plantation he became a newspaper man, winning a fine reputation because of his willingness to make the most of whatever opportunity came his way.

This book will tell you how it happened, entirely by accident as Mr. Harris thought, that he finally came to be a writer of books known and loved all over the world. But it was no accident. There would have been no "Uncle Remus" stories if the boy Joel Harris hadn't discovered the fulness of life in the world that lay about him.

When I take visitors to the memorial room in the Emory University Library, and show them the yellowed sheets on which Joel Chandler Harris wrote the stories of Uncle Remus and of life in Middle Georgia, I like to begin by telling about his boyhood at Turnwold, for it all began there. Wordsworth said that "The child is father of the man." It was so in Joel Chandler Harris's case. His was a useful life, and a happy life, because he never stopped to think that any part of it might be dull.

Thomas H. English
Curator, Joel Chandler Harris Collection
Emory University
February 1941

JOEL CHANDLER HARRIS

PLANTATION STORYTELLER

CHAPTER ONE

Old Sis Goose

ONE balmy late April afternoon, many years ago, Mrs. Leverette and her out-of-town guest were sitting on the former's front porch in the little town of Eatonton, in middle Georgia. Suddenly a pebble crashed through the young foliage of a maple tree just outside the front fence, sending birds flying in all directions.

"Mercy on us!" exclaimed the nervous guest, with a start. Another pebble, with deadly aim, hit a knothole in the tree. A yellow-brown dog of marvelously mixed ancestry thrust his nose between the bars of the gate, beaming and wagging his tail at the ladies on the porch. A small, redheaded, barefoot boy followed close behind him, whistling.

"Hello, Joel!" greeted Mrs. Leverette, her face, which had been rather stern, relaxing somewhat.

"Howdy, Miz Leverette!" he returned, grinning infectiously.

"It's Joel Harris," explained Mrs. Leverette to her guest, "and his dog, Brutus—or Brute, as Joel calls him. The youngster is so mischievous, he's rather a trial sometimes, but you can't be angry with him long.

"He and his mother live in that little cottage there next to us. His father ran off and deserted them here, and we only know that he is supposed to have gone to California with the Gold Rush. Joel's mother had a hard time at first, and if the folks here hadn't all pitched in and helped her, I don't know what would have become of her. But we just couldn't sit around and see the poor young thing suffer.

"Well, she was as brave as could be. She began taking in sewing, and she has supported herself and Joel that way ever since; doesn't ask any odds of anybody. Mr. Andrew Reid—he's the man who built this house we live in, you know—and his family took such a liking to her that he handed over to her that little cottage next door, for her home. She didn't want to take it, for she's awfully independent."

"Did he actually give it to her?"

"No, just loaned it to her for as long as she wants it. After Mr. Reid moved across town and we came here, we grew very fond of her. My husband loves to get into an argument with her on politics or something else, and she's often a match for him, too. He says her mind is so keen that contact with it sharpens his own."

"How long has she been here?" asked the friend.

"Well, I remember it was campaign year when she came; the year they elected old General Taylor president."

"That was 1848."

"Yes, and Joel was born in December after the election. That makes him—let's see—eight and a half years old. He's a funny little fellow; small for his years, and full of mischief, but bright as a new dollar, and you can't help liking him."

Meanwhile, Joel's mother had returned from the post

office and found her mother—who had come from the old home to visit her for a few days—alone.

"Joel went over to see his old Negro friend, Uncle Bob Capers," explained his grandmother. "He said Uncle Bob had hurt his hand and isn't working today."

Mrs. Harris smiled. "And Uncle Bob," she said, "will spin some more of those endless yarns of his about the animals—Brother Fox and Brother Rabbit and Brother Bear and the rest of them, as if they were all members of his Baptist church." Then a look of concern came over her face. "I wonder if Uncle Bob is badly hurt."

"Oh, I guess not, from what Joel said. Just an excuse to take a day's layoff," said the older woman. She paused to count stitches in her knitting, and then went on, "Some of the old Negroes over in Newton County tell those animal stories, too. I wonder where they get them?"

"I haven't any idea, I'm sure," replied her daughter, sitting down at a table. "Now excuse me for a moment, Mother. I must make out a bill for Mr. Turner. He's that rich planter and lawyer I've told you about; lives northeast of here. I've just finished making a suit of clothes for him."

"Does he do his lawing out on his farm?" asked the mother.

"No, he and his brother, Mr. William Turner, have an office here in town, and they take turns coming in to it. Mr. William is in the office some days in the week, and Mr. Joseph the other days. Mr. Joseph is my customer. He gives me some good orders now and then. He supplies the cloth, and I make the things.

"People seem to think," she added as an afterthought,

"that neither one of the brothers cares much about law. They are both literary."

She dipped her pen in the ink, which she herself had made from powdered oak galls and iron rust, mixed with water in which there was a little vinegar, and made out the bill:

Eatonton, Ga.,
April 23, 1857.

Mr. J. A. Turner

to Mrs. Mary Harris, Dr.

1 coat	$2.50
1 pr. pants	1.50
1 vest	1.00
4 shirts	4.00
	$9.00

"So you think you'll never come back to Newton County to live," said the older woman after awhile.

"No, Mother," replied her daughter. "I've made a place for Joel and myself here, the people have been very kind and understanding, and I don't want to go back there, where I made the worst mistake of my life. But here's what I've been thinking. The family at home are all gone now, and someday soon, instead of my coming to live with you, I want you to come and live with me." And that was what came to pass a few years later.

Meanwhile, over at Uncle Bob Capers' little cabin, a short distance away, the old Negro and Joel sat talking on the tiny front porch. Uncle Bob was a teamster and drove a wagon for the cotton mill, Eatonton's only factory, and that not a very large one. He often let Joel ride on the wagon seat with him. He now sat with his bruised hand tied up in a rag, and smoked his cob pipe with great enjoyment.

"I been usin' coon grease on it," said he, referring to his hand, "and I reckon by tomorrer or nex' day, hit'll be so I kin go to work again."

Joel, a slender little boy with red hair, rather large mouth, merry blue eyes, and a face covered with freckles, sat beside him. He was already barefoot—most boys in the country went barefoot all summer then—for the weather is mild in middle Georgia in late April, and it was necessary to save shoes whenever possible. His clothes were homemade, his shirt of calico and his trousers of blue cottonade, both faded and carefully mended. He was much interested in telling of a goose which he had seen down by the pond.

"It was standing on one foot with the other held up against its body so I couldn't see it," he said, "and it stood there and stood there and stood there, as long as I was watching it. I guess it must've been a half an hour. I don't see how it could stand that long on one foot. Why do they do that, Uncle Bob?"

"Well, suh," said Uncle Bob slowly, trying to think of an answer so that his reputation for wisdom would not suffer, "when dey does dat, it's giner'ly because dey want to rest de odder foot—des like I restin' dis right hand today." He held it up.

"Sometimes that goose had its eyes shut, while I was watching it," said Joel. "Do they ever sleep all night on one leg?"

"As to dat," said Uncle Bob, "dey might stan' on one foot and forgit deyself and drap off in a doze. But at night dey sets down on de ground, honey; sets down de same as you doin' right now. Co'se dey don't cross de'r legs," he added, with another glance at the little boy, "ca'se dey sets down right flat-footed.

"Dese hyer gooses is mighty cu'ious fowls," he continued, crumpling some leaf tobacco and cramming it into his pipe. "Dey sho is cu'ious."

Joel knew that a story was coming. He leaned forward in his chair and waited eagerly.

"In old times de gooses was 'mongst de big bugs," Uncle Bob went on, "and when ole Miss Goose went a-dinin', de quality was dere. Likewise, needer was dey stuck up, ca'se wid all de'r carryin' on, Miss Goose weren't too proud fur to take in washin' fur de neighborhoods, an' she made money an' got fat an' slick.

"Dis de way matters stan' when one day Br'er Fox and Br'er Rabbit, dey was settin' up at de cotton patch, one on one side de fence, an' t'er one on t'er side, gwine on wid one anodder, when fust news dey know, dey hear somep'n —*blim! blim! blim!*

"Br'er Fox, he ax what dat fuss is, an' Br'er Rabbit, he up an' 'spon' dat it's ole Sis Goose down at de spring. Br'er Fox, he up'n' ax what she doin', an' Br'er Rabbit, he say, says he, dat she battlin' clo'es."

The old man did not need to tell Joel the meaning of "battling clothes." In those days there were no washing machines nor even corrugated washboards. The common way of laundering was to wet and soap the clothes, then lay them on a block of wood or a heavy plank and pound them with a paddle called a "battling stick," which drove the suds all through the cloth. Unless the washerwoman was careful, the process might be pretty hard on buttons.

"When Br'er Fox hear dat," continued Uncle Bob, "he

Joel knew that a story was coming. He leaned forward in his chair and waited eagerly.

sorter lick his chops, an' 'low dat some o' dese odd-come-shorts he gwine to call an' pay his 'spects. De minute he say dat, Br'er Rabbit, he know dat somep'n was up, an he 'low hisself dat he 'spect he better whirl in an' have some fun whiles it gwine on. By'm'by Br'er Fox up'n' say to Br'er Rabbit dat he bleedged to be movin' 'long tow'ds home, an' wid dat dey bofe say good-by.

"Br'er Fox, he put out to whar his fambly was, but Br'er Rabbit, he slip 'round, he did, an' call on ole Miss Goose —ole Miss Goose, down at de spring, washin' an' b'ilin' an' battlin' clo'es. Br'er Rabbit he march up an' ax her howdy, an' den she tuck'n' ax Br'er Rabbit howdy.

" 'I'd shake hands 'long wid you, Br'er Rabbit,' says she, 'but dey're all full o' suds,' says she.

" 'No matter 'bout dat, Sis Goose,' says Br'er Rabbit, says he, 'so long as yo' will's good,' says he."

"Miss Goose—with hands?" exclaimed Joel, startled, despite the fact that he had heard many curious things about animals from Uncle Bob before.

"How you know goose ain't got hands?" Uncle Bob demanded, with a frown. "Is you been sleepin' longer'n old man Know-All? Little mo', an' you'll up an' stan' me down dat snakes ain't got no foots, an' yit you take an' lay a snake down in front o' de fire, an' his foots'll come out right befo' yo' eyes."

After a slightly offended pause, he continued:

"Atter old Miss Goose an' Br'er Rabbit done pass de time o' day wid one anodder, Br'er Rabbit, he ax her, he did, how she come on dese days, an' Miss Goose say, mighty po'ly.

" 'I's gittin' stiff an' I's gittin' clumsy,' says she, 'an' mo'n dat, I's gittin' blind,' says she. 'Des 'fo' you happen along, Br'er Rabbit, I drap my specks in de tub hyer, an' if you'd 'a' come along 'bout dat time,' says ole Miss Goose, says she, 'I lay I'd 'a' tuck you for dat nasty, owdacious Br'er Fox, an' it'd 'a' been a born blessin' if I hadn't 'a' scald you wid a pan o' b'ilin suds,' says she. 'I'm dat glad I found my specks, I dunno w'at to do,' says ole Miss Goose, says she.

"Den Br'er Rabbit, he up'n say dat bein's how Sis Goose done fotch up Br'er Fox's name, he got somep'n for to tell her, an' den he let out 'bout Br'er Fox gwine to call on her.

" 'He comin', says Br'er Rabbit, says he; 'he comin', sho' an' when he come, hit'll be des 'fo' day,' says he.

"Wid dat, ole Miss Goose wipe her han's on her apern, an' put her specks up on her for'ead, an' look like she done got trouble on 'er mind.

" 'Laws-a-massy!' says she. ' 'Sposen he come, Br'er Rabbit! W'at I gwine do? An' dey ain't a man 'bout de house, needer,' says she.

"Br'er Rabbit, he shut one eye, an' he say, says he:

" 'Sis Goose, de time done come when you 'bleedged to roost high. You look like you got de dropsy,' says he, 'but don't mind dat, ca'se if you don't roost high, you're a goner,' says he.

"Den ole Miss Goose ax Br'er Rabbit w'at she gwine do, an' Br'er Rabbit he up'n tell her dat she must go home an' tie up a bundle o' de white folks' clo'es an' put 'em on de bed, an' den she must fly up on a rafter an' let Br'er Fox grab de clo'es and run off wid 'em.

"Ole Miss Goose say she much 'bliged, an' she tuck'n tuck her things an' waddle off home; an' dat night she do like Br'er Rabbit say wid de bundle o' clo'es, an' den she sent word to Mr. Dog, an' Mr. Dog he come down an' say he'd sorter set up wid her.

"Des 'fo' day, hyer come Br'er Fox creepin' up, an' he

went an' push on de do' easy, an' de do' open, an' he see somep'n white on de bed which he tuck for Miss Goose, an' he grab it an' run. 'Bout dat time, Mr. Dog sail out f'm under de house, he did, an if Br'er Fox hadn't drapt de clo'es, he'd 'a' got cotched. F'm dat, word went 'roun' dat Br'er Fox been tryin' to steal Miss Goose's clo'es, an' he come mighty nigh losin' his standin' at Miss Meadows's. Down to dis day," Uncle Bob concluded, knocking the ashes out of his pipe, "Br'er Fox b'lieve dat Br'er Rabbit was de 'casion o' Mr. Dog bein' in de neighborhoods at dat time o' night, an' Br'er Rabbit ain't 'spute it. De bad feelin' 'twixt Br'er Fox an' Mr. Dog start right den an' dar, an' hit's been gwine on, till now dey ain't git in smellin' distance o' one anodder widout dey's a row."

CHAPTER TWO

Little Red-Head

WHEN Joel was about six years old, his mother sent him to a little "subscription" school in the village—which means that the parent paid the teacher a dollar a month for the child's tuition. There were no public schools then, such as we have now. But there was a somewhat better school in Eatonton, called an academy, and after a year or two, Mr. Andrew Reid—who had loaned Mrs. Harris her cottage home—suggested that Joel be sent there. The tuition was higher, but Mr. Reid asked that he be permitted to pay it. Mrs. Harris was very reluctant to accept this favor, but she yearned so greatly for an education for her boy that she finally overcame her scruples for his sake.

Joel's teacher and schoolmates remembered in after years that he never seemed to study very hard, and yet he nearly always had his lessons learned as well as anybody, or better. His teachers all agreed that he had a very quick mind.

When he was nine years old, he and his fellow pupils were asked by the teacher to write a composition on a subject which they themselves might choose. This was Joel's:

The Elephant
The Elephant is one of the largest animals that lives on land. Elephants. live wild in Asia. Some are caught and tamed and after they are tamed they are very obedient to their master, They will never forget an unkind act done to them by by any person, They are very sagacious and can understand whatever their master. tells Them to do

Joel C Harris

In the next two or three years, the teachers began saying that Joel was the best composition writer in his grade.

Joel was not strong enough to hold his own in the rough-and-tumble scuffling which the other boys indulged in, and he didn't care for that sort of play, anyhow. But playing with tops and marbles or with animals, playing jokes, hunting, roving in the woods and fields—he found much fun in these. He would have had more dogs than Brutus if his mother had permitted it.

"And cats!" she exclaimed in despair to a neighbor. "You don't know anyone who needs a cat, do you? I don't know what I am to do with the stray kittens that Joel brings in. I've just had to put my foot down and tell him flatly that he mustn't bring any more."

Brutus was a loyal playfellow, but like all country dogs, the nights were full of excitement for him. A person who visits in the country often wonders when the dogs get any sleep at all. Some of them bark most of the night, others have a habit of howling at times, especially if the moon is shining. We can only surmise that they think they are singing. Brutus's favorite spot for doing this was squarely under Mrs. Harris's bedroom window.

"I can't imagine why he insists upon serenading me," she said. "I certainly don't appreciate it."

Shouting at him did no good. He would cease for the time being, but a few nights later, he would forget himself and be at it again. Finally, in desperation, Mrs. Harris filled a pan with stones and pieces of brick, and that night, while Brutus was in the midst of his solo, she leaned from the window and emptied it on his back. He fled yelping around the house, but he took the hint, and never warbled under her window again.

Joel had a playmate, Charlie Leonard, with whom he contrived to get into no little mischief. There was a younger brother, Jim Leonard, but Charlie was more nearly of Joel's age and was his favorite pal. Together they ranged all over town and into the surrounding country; fishing and swimming as they grew older, hunting rabbits, hunting wild plums, wild strawberries, nuts, persimmons, wild grapes.

A much-loved play-place was the White Mud Gullies, deep ditches, almost like small canyons, cut in the soil during rainy weather. Their name indicated that their color was a peculiarity; most of the soil in that part of Georgia was dark red. In the curves of these little chasms, which seemed immense to small boys, one could fancy almost any great adventure happening. Indians, bandits, giants, gnomes, knights in armor, Robin Hood—the reading which Joel was doing at an early age supplied him with all sorts of wonderful beings to imagine stealing or charging through those depths.

Also, quite near the White Mud Gullies lived Aunt
Betsy Cuthbert, an old colored woman who was a famous
cook. She was a cherished friend of the two boys, of whom
she was equally fond. Joel and Charlie, when they were
small, often played with her grandchildren. When they
heard Aunt Betsy call them, they came scrambling out of
the ditches like mad, for they knew that she was apt to have
a treat ready for them.

"I des got thoo bakin' some ginger cakes," she would say,
"an' I thought you might like a little to sorter stay yo'
stommicks until de next meal." Or it might be some of
her remarkable potato biscuits and butter, or a flat chicken
pie, another of her specialities. Everything she made was
good.

On Saturday mornings, when they were eleven and
twelve years old, Joel would come over to the Leonard
home, where Charlie and Jim had a certain number of
chores to do—hoeing in the garden, sweeping the bare
places in the backyard, and so on—before they could get
away for their Saturday play. Joel would sit on the fence
and tease them while they toiled, until in exasperation they
would throw clods at him. No doubt there was much less
work done because of his presence. But in a little while the
job would be over, and then Joel or Charlie would say,
"Le's go rabbit hunting," and away they would dash.

Jim, though much younger, always wanted to tag along.
But his legs were so much shorter that he could not keep
up with the other two, and at such times they considered
him a nuisance. If he insisted on going, they had a method
of getting rid of him. Joel would grab him and hold him,
while Charlie ran across fields at top speed. Then when
Charlie had got a good start, Joel would throw Jim's hat

into a big rose bush or over a fence and run, too. A boy of those days didn't feel that he could go anywhere outdoors without a hat. As Joel could run like a deer, by the time Jim had recovered his hat, the other two would be too far away for him to catch.

There were many well-to-do planters in Putnam County then. One of them was Mr. Harvey Dennis, whose big farm lay on the outskirts of Eatonton. He was very fond of Joel, though the youngster was sometimes rather a trial to him. He always kept eight or ten hounds for fox hunting, his favorite sport. But a fox hound will follow a rabbit trail, too, if taken out in daylight and encouraged to do so. So the boys would go down along a brook in a little glen near Mr. Dennis's home, where they would call in a guarded tone and clap their hands to attract the attention of his dogs. The sounds were seldom heard by the human beings around the house, but the keen-eared dogs heard them, and knew that the boys were waiting for them. Always eager for the chase, away they went, and the boys would quickly hear the musical *"Ouf! ouf! ouf!"* of their baying as they galloped down the hill with wildly flapping ears.

Then with the dogs—always including Brutus, of course —bouncing happily around them, the boys would hurry away over the rolling country, past the little hut of Aunt Betsy Cole, a noted fortune teller, who lived alone and was very fascinating to the boys. With her bent figure, wrinkled face, hooked nose and sunken lips, it was easy for them to fancy her a witch, and the fact that she lived very close to the town cemetery made this seem more probable. The boys often lingered a little at her place, to catch a glimpse of her if they could.

Once when she was puttering about her little yard, they stood staring, round-eyed, over the fence at her until she became angry.

"What are you young-uns gawpin' at?" she shrilled. "Don't your folks teach you no manners? Go on about your business!"

"Old witch!" shouted Charlie daringly.

At that she was furious. She came hobbling, as fast as she could, through the gate, brandishing her stick, calling them "owdacious little varmints" and other names, while they ran for dear life.

There was a rabbit—the boys believed it was always the same one—which they saw and chased several times near the cemetery. Twice, when they first caught sight of it, it was sitting on its haunches, putting its forepaws up to its nose.

"Look, it's spitting on its hands," Joel would say, "Now we'll never catch it."

And they never did.

"That's because it's a graveyard rabbit," said Charlie. "They're smarter than any other kind."

(Those superstitious folk, even to this day, who carry a rabbit's foot, think that to be effective in bringing luck, it must be the left hind foot of a graveyard rabbit.)

"Do you know what, Charlie?" said Joel one day. "That rabbit is Aunt Betsy Cole. You know witches can change themselves into animals whenever they want to."

Small boys often like to make themselves believe such things, and this was particularly apt to be true in a rustic community in Georgia eighty or ninety years ago.

They finally ceased to spend much time in trying to catch the graveyard rabbit, and would hurry on to Colonel

"You boys have got my dogs again," he said reproachfully.

Nicholson's plantation, which was their favorite hunting ground.

Sometime during the forenoon, Mr. Dennis was apt to notice the absence of the hounds and say, "Those boys have toled off my dogs again." It annoyed him, for if the dogs hunted rabbits with the boys, they might get into the habit of following rabbit scent when he took them fox hunting. Now and then, if he had time, he would saddle his horse and follow them, for he could be pretty sure that they had gone to Colonel Nicholson's farm. If he caught up with them, he was never rough or angry in his manner. He would just sit on his horse, looking at them reproachfully, and say, "You boys have got my dogs again."

"But Mr. Dennis," Joel would say in his usual respectful manner toward older people, "we'll give you the rabbits we catch."

"That's very kind of you," Mr. Dennis would retort with gentle sarcasm, "but I don't want my dogs spoiled for fox hunting."

They did give him many rabbits, and Mr. Dennis could never be greatly out of humor with them.

"Boys will be boys," he would say resignedly. He liked Joel and saw that he was an unusual boy. "That Harris youngster is going to surprise the world one of these days," was his opinion.

Joel and Charlie gladly trailed along when he went gunning, and carried his game; and when he wanted to train his young dogs for fox hunting, or keep the older ones in good trim, he would let the boys take a fox skin and drag it through woods and fields for two miles or more—over fences and other obstacles and across brooks. The boys enjoyed this sport greatly.

"Don't it sound funny," Charlie would say, as they stopped to listen, "to hear them old dogs carryin' on just like they were after a real fox?"

"As smart as those dogs are," said Joel, "you'd think they would learn to tell the difference between the scent of a live fox and a dead hide, but they never do."

Finally, when the hounds got too close upon their heels, the boys would scramble up a tree. This was to keep the dogs from tearing the fox skin to pieces and perhaps injuring the boys themselves in their excitement at making the catch. There the youngsters would roost, with the dogs baying around the foot of the tree until Mr. Dennis came and called them off.

In peach season Mr. Dennis sometimes called the two boys into his orchard and gave them all the peaches they could carry. Naturally, they thought him one of the finest of men, and eventually, as they grew older, they became ashamed to take his dogs out on frolics against his wishes.

One of the pupils in the academy was a boy known as "Hut" Adams, who was about four years older than either Joel or Charlie, but who seemed to prefer associating with them instead of with boys of his own age, and he frequently led them into pranks which they might not have thought of otherwise. The academy was on the farther side of town from where these three lived. They might go to and from it either through the main street or by a slight detour across some vacant lots called the Commons. Early in September, when they came out of school in the afternoon, Hut would sometimes say to the younger boys, "Let's go home by the Commons."

They usually knew what that meant. Going that way,

they passed near Mr. Edmund Reid's peach orchard and watermelon patch. Hut would slip through the fence and get a watermelon, perhaps some peaches, too, and pass them out to the smaller boys. Two or three times Mr. Reid saw them and gave chase. He was a wealthy and good-natured man and had more fruit than he could use, and the townsfolk used to say that he chased the boys just for fun of seeing them run for dear life, their short legs taking four steps to his one, dropping the melon and often some of the peaches, too, in their efforts to lighten ballast. That Mr. Reid never complained to their parents seems to prove that he didn't take these affairs very seriously.

On summer Sunday afternoons, Charlie and Joel liked to go to the brook—they called it the "branch"—near Joel's house, and Hut Adams often stole away and joined them, though his father was a prominent church member and insisted that his family and his servants must observe Sunday by refraining from all amusements. Hut was the only one of the three boys who carried a handkerchief, and he let the others use it as a seine in their efforts to catch minnows in the deeper pools.

Joel dearly loved to play jokes, and one of his favorite victims was Hut, though he always had to run like mad afterward, for Hut was so much bigger than he was that he could whip Joel without half trying.

Hut liked to be a showman, too, and would promote what he called the "Gully Minstrels," their theater being a certain place in the White Mud Gullies. Hut was the manager, Joel the principal comedian, and Charlie the treasurer. The price of admission was ten pins—the favorite childhood currency of those days, when few children had any real money. The minstrels were well patronized; sometimes they had audiences of six or eight, mostly little girls. But as it always happened, they presently found themselves with a quantity of pins on hand and nothing they could do with them, so the Gully Minstrels would disband for several weeks or months, until Hut felt the urge to start them going again.

Joel's dearest loafing place of all was Mr. McDade's livery stable. There are so few livery stables nowadays that it may be well to explain that it was in part a sort of horse hotel, where you could leave your horse and vehicle, to be boarded and cared for as long as you liked. The livery stable also had horses and vehicles of its own, which might be rented by the hour or day.

More than once Joel and Charlie played hooky from school for days on end and hung around the livery stable the whole time. It was not on the main street, and therefore their parents were not apt to come by—though they kept a sharp lookout lest one of the familiar figures should appear. They sometimes played in the hayloft, but the principal attraction to them was the association with horses.

Mr. McDade liked them, and he would let them ride the horses to a brook near by for a drink of water, or to the blacksmith's shop.

"Boys," he would say, "take these two horses over to the shop and tell Henry I want 'em shod with kinder light shoes all around. They're buggy hosses, and I want 'em so they can pick up their feet and go. Tell him to remember that that sorrel interferes with her hind feet a little, and make his shoes accordin'ly."

The boys always remembered these instructions to the letter. Leading the horses alongside the railing of the stalls, they would climb up the planks and onto their backs.

"Why, the blacksmith's shop is just across the street," perhaps a stranger would say. "Why don't they just lead them over?"

"Mister," the liveryman would reply, with a laugh, "if them boys was goin' to carry them hosses no mo' than twenty feet, they'd git on their backs and ride."

The drovers and plantation owners in the vicinity had some very fine animals, and it was a great honor for the boys to ride these horses when they were left in the stable overnight or perhaps for several days while their owners were in town attending court sessions. Another great treat was a trip on a wagon with their old pal, Uncle Ben Sadler, Negro hostler at the stable, when he went to the country at intervals to bring in corn and fodder.

With all this experience, Joel very early became something of an expert in handling horses. His mother was appalled one day, when he was no more than ten years old, to see him tooling along the streets of Eatonton beside the driver of the mail stage, holding the reins of the spirited team with the skill and nonchalance of a veteran coachman.

There were moments when some folk in Eatonton doubted that Joel would ever come to any good end, and even predicted that he would wind up in the penitentiary. There was the affair of the hogs, for example. Men who rode into town from the country usually tied their horses to the hitching rack, a long pole set horizontally across the tops of some posts on one side of the courthouse square. The stamping of the horses' forefeet in wet weather churned the earth near the rack into mudholes. In these the hogs—which ran at large in both small town and city in those days—loved to lie and wallow.

One day, just after a heavy rain, when the mud was particularly nice, several horses were hitched to the rack, and some hogs were lying in the mud, almost under them. Joel, passing by, saw opportunity for some fun. He picked up two or three stones, and in rapid succession hurled them at the fat sides of the porkers. As they reached their targets, the hogs sprang up with loud *"Oink! oink! oinks!"* of pained terror and ran, bumping into the horses' legs and throwing them into a panic. They jerked backward, breaking the hitch reins, and fled, galloping in all directions through the streets. Some even ran out into the country, leaving their riders marooned, while Joel, appalled at the havoc he had created, ran down a side street, but not before he had been noticed and his doom on the gallows predicted by some of the elders of the town.

CHAPTER THREE

The Old Scrapbook

UT there was another side to Joel, a curious contrast to his love of play and nonsense. We find these two contrasting phases in many persons of talent. Joel believed in after years that his desire to write, to give expression on paper to his thoughts, grew out of hearing his mother read Oliver Goldsmith's novel, *The Vicar of Wakefield*. He was very young at the time—he couldn't remember afterward how young. His grandmother sat on the other side of the fire while Mrs. Harris read—she had come to visit them at the time—and Joel sat between them, listening attentively. He was too young to grasp the full meaning of what was going on in the story, though he followed it pretty well. But literary appreciation had begun to appear in him even at that early age, for, as he later wrote:

> There was something in the style or something in the humor of that remarkable little book that struck my fancy, and I straightway fell to composing little tales in which the principal character, whether hero or heroine, silenced the other characters by crying "Fudge!" at every possible oppor-

tunity. None of these little tales have been preserved, but I am convinced that since their keynote was "Fudge!" they must have been very close to human nature.

Style and humor! Those were the two things which marked the work of Joel Chandler Harris in his writing career. *The Vicar of Wakefield* doesn't waste words; it tells its story tersely, and that came to be Joel's way of writing, too. He had a little later, as we shall see, a critic who impressed this idea still more forcibly upon him. And as for the "Fudge!" Joel found that in *The Vicar of Wakefield,* too. There is one grumpy character in the book, a Mr. Burchell, who sits through a whole chapter sneeringly crying "Fudge!" at everything said by anybody else. That struck Joel as enormously funny.

The first book that Joel owned was a small *Life of General Zachary Taylor,* who, by the way, was elected President of the United States just a month before Joel was born. This little volume was given him by his teacher when he was not yet six years old (he had begun going to school at five), and he kept it all his life.

Mary Harris continued her reading aloud as Joel grew older, often choosing books which were a little beyond his understanding, though he never failed to get something out of them. It wasn't long before he began to do the reading himself, and he read more and more as the years passed. His mother had little or no money with which to buy books, magazines, and newspapers, but many of these were loaned to her by friends, and Joel began to devour them long before he could pronounce many of the words.

It came to be hard for him to decide which he liked best—reading or the out of doors, with its dogs and horses, and—well, there were other things, too. Those hours of listening, for example, to Uncle Bob and Aunt Betsy tell their quaint stories of the animals, and why guinea fowls are "speckledy," and how the ocean was made, not to mention fearsome tales about witches and ghosts.

"Where did you hear all these things about the animals, Uncle Bob?" Joel asked once.

"Well, my granddaddy, he tol' most of 'em to me," said Uncle Bob, " 'cept'n some I hear f'm odder ole men. An' dey hear 'em f'm men older dan dey is—an' dat's de way it goes, plumb back to ole man Know-All; he de fust man to tell 'em, I speck, ca'se he knowed all de animals, an' could talk to 'em in dey own languidge."

Joel could never learn anything more from him about this old man Know-All; he was a very mysterious character.

There was another person in town who interested Joel greatly, and who, in turn, was interested in him. This was a lawyer with the strange name of Demetrios. He had an office in one of the rooms of the old tavern; a large room whose windows looked out on the porch, with its long row of wooden columns. His bedroom was immediately adjoining it. His name was so long that nearly everybody in Eatonton, Joel among them, just called him Mr. Deo. He was short and inclined to be fat, and wore side-whiskers, which gave him quite a different appearance from the other men in town, for the fashion then was to wear either a full beard or a mustache with what was called a goatee, though young men often got along for several years with the mustache alone.

Mr. Deo spoke with a very slight foreign pronunciation. Many people did not notice it, but Joel did, because he listened so much to the plump little man's conversation, and because, even in boyhood, he became a close observer of speech. That was what later made him a wonderful writer of dialect.

Mr. Deo was a native of Greece, and though he said little about his past, it was rumored in town that he had had to leave his homeland on account of politics, for Greece was frequently in turmoil in the first half of the nineteenth century. As Joel wrote of himself in later years, "Joe didn't know until long afterward that politics could be a crime. He thought that politics consisted largely in newspaper articles signed 'Old Subscriber,' or 'Many Citizens,' or 'Vox Populi,' or 'Scrutator,' and partly in arguments between the men who sat in fine weather on the drygoods boxes under the china trees."

One of Joel's first memories of Mr. Deo was that of hearing Mr. Leverette telling his mother one evening of an exciting event on the Courthouse Square that day. An important trial was in progress, and Mr. Demetrios was one of the attorneys.

"He put Bill Ashurst on the stand, and just turned him inside out," said Mr. Leverette. "Made Bill contradict himself and try to lie out of it until he was a laughingstock. Got Bill so mad that the judge threatened to fine him for contempt. When the session was over, Mr. Deo came down the steps of the courthouse, and Bill met him on the sidewalk and spat in his face."

"My conscience!" exclaimed Mrs. Harris. "What did Mr. Deo do?"

"He just stood a moment, smiling at Bill while he took out his handkerchief, and wiped his face. Then he walked across to his office, wrote out a challenge to a duel, and sent it to Bill by a messenger. The last I heard, about half an hour ago, Bill hadn't answered it yet."

He never did answer it, and to flunk a challenge in the South in those days was apt to be deadly to a man's reputation. Mr. Deo had many friends in Eatonton who thought he was in the right, and he gained more friends by not publicly denouncing Ashurst as a coward, as was often done in such a case, but just by keeping silent about the matter. Ashurst, however, heard so many sneers at his cowardice in the next few months that he left Putnam County for good and settled somewhere in the West.

By the time he was eleven years old, Joel had made Mr. Deo's acquaintance and became a frequent visitor at his office. Mr. Deo was a good attorney and a fine public speaker, and the men of the town, especially the other lawyers, liked him and thought him so interesting that it was only occasionally that Joel could find him in his office alone. But the boy never seemed to be considered an intruder. "Come in, Joe," was the hearty greeting he always received, even though there were others present. Because of the mystery of his past, it pleased Joel to imagine all sorts of romantic things about him. How in the world did a man from far-off Greece happen to stray into a little country town in Georgia? That is a question which never was answered.

Once when the two were alone in the office, Mr. Deo went into his bedroom, took from a closet a military uniform, and put it on. Joel though it was the most beautiful costume he had ever seen. Gold braid ran down the side of the trousers, there were gold cords draped in curves across the front of the coat, and a pair of big gold-fringed

Joel thought it was the most beautiful costume he had ever seen.

epaulets crowned each shoulder. The hat was somewhat like those Joel had seen pictured in books. It was gold-edged, the brim at the sides was turned up and fastened with little gold buttons, and a shining black feather trailed over the top of it. Short and fat though he was, Mr. Deo looked very handsome to Joel in this gorgeous outfit. He would not tell when or where he wore it, which gave Joel opportunity for some more romantic imaginings.

"It was in Europe a long time ago," was all he would say. "Yes, I have seen war; too much war, Joe."

Mr. Deo had some boxes in his room, and when Joel discovered that they were full of books, he was so plainly eager to see them that Mr. Deo said, "You may look through them if you like. But be sure to put them all back before you go. Don't leave any strewn around."

Joel promised, and dug into the boxes day after day, ransacking them to the very bottom—sometimes scarcely aware that Mr. Deo and other men were sitting in the room talking. Many of the books were printed in a strange sort of type; he had never seen anything like it before.

"It is Greek—my own language," Mr. Deo smiled. He picked up a volume. "You have heard about the siege of Troy and Hector and Achilles and all the other heroes, have you not?"

"Oh yes, sir."

"Well, here is the story, just as it was originally written—by a Greek poet named Homer twenty-five hundred years or more ago; we don't know just how long." He let the volume fall open at random, and pointing at the words with his pencil, he translated the narrative of the combat between Pandarus, Diomedes and Aeneas. Joel sat spell-bound. It scarcely seemed possible that that thrilling story could be contained in these outlandish-looking "chicken tracks."

"There are many other books here that you will not be able to read," said Mr. Deo. "Books in Latin, French, and Italian."

Joel looked at him, awe-stricken. "Can you read them all?" he asked.

"Yes, fairly well," Mr. Deo smiled again at him. "After you have learned two or three languages, the rest are easier, for they are all related."

Joel also found many books in English, all printed long, long ago. A history of Europe, and one of England, *Poems by Mr. Gray,* a queer little story called *Rasselas* "by Dr. Johnson"—Joel supposed that he was a doctor of medicine until Mr. Deo set him aright. Mr. Deo let him take some of them home.

Then there were the evenings at the Leverettes' home, next door, which were highly entertaining. The two families were such close friends that Mr. Leverette had made a gate in the fence between, so that they could pass back and forth more easily. Joel and his mother were frequently invited over by their kindly neighbors to eat supper or spend the evening, and at such times Mr. Leverette delighted in stirring up Mary Harris by starting a controversy on politics or religion or any other subject that came handy. Finding on which side she stood, he would pretend to lean toward the other side, to draw her out. She was usually a match for him in argument, which did not annoy him at all. Instead, he enjoyed her quick retorts, her fund of information and intelligent opinion.

"And so you think this book, *The Impending Crisis,* is a true picture of slavery?" he might say.

"Not entirely," she would reply, "but I think it has more truth in it than we Southerners are willing to admit. I believe the crisis is more serious than we realize." And away they would go, hammer and tongs.

But life was not all play and reading for Joel. He had chores to do at home—hoeing vegetables and chasing potato bugs and helping his mother with her flower garden, which was the most genial task of all.

It is hard to say when he first began trying to write; perhaps when he was not more than ten years old. He was not yet twelve when he began scribbling crude poems and stories, and then little boyish essays in an old blank book which he found lying about the house. Most of them were unfinished. "Tiger, or the Passo de Real," "Allie Graham, or the Broken Heart," "The Indian's Revenge"—they all show the influence of the brightly colored popular fiction of the day, which always had adorable heroines and heroes with the courage of lions. Some of them are signed "Harris" or "Marlowe," a pen name which he thought of adopting. In "The Comanche's Daughter; a Tale of North Mexico, by Marlowe," the hero, upon hearing his mother pronounce the name of Rose Norton, who had been kidnaped by the Indians, "started, turned pale and clenched his fists, while his eyes fairly shot fire"—all of which was in the best popular style.

"The Bandit King" was probably first of all to be put down on paper. It starts off with a dreadful error in grammar, and the spelling is at times below par:

The Bandit King

And this then was the famous & daring bandit of the Appennines. Yes, it was him. He had the appearance of being about thirty five years of age. He was of giant stature, somewhat thin and symetrycal. . . . His dress consisted of a wolf-skin cap, the tail of which hung over his right shoulder; a dress coat of blue cashmere with gold buttons across the breast; pants of the same material with gold braid down the seam. A buck-skin belt was around his waist, and the butts of two revolvers could be seen protruding from behind the belt; also the silver handle of the far-famed Italian stilletto. A carbine hung to his back by a leather strap. Every time he would move his left hand, I could see the flashing of a jewelled ring on his little finger. His face was almost girlish in its expression . . . elegant, not dark like the rest of his daring band. His nose was neither of Roman structure or of Aquiline—just enough of both to be beautifull. His cheeks were of a rosy hue with pouting lips of a cherry red. His eyes were black and glittering & if it were not for his eyes I should have said he was an American. . . . His manners were dignified and gracefull to all, even to the lowest menial in his band. . . . He was neither Haghty nor indolent. This then was the celebrated bandit robber Guilermo of the Mountains & I was the captive of this man. It was said he was extremely benevolent to the poor giving to them half of what he took from the rich.

But though the writer was the captive of Guilermo, the bandit treated him hospitably in his mountain lair, and finally revealed to him that he, Guilermo, was really an American. As Joel rushed on to the end of the story, he completely forgot all about punctuation:

"You see this ring," said he & his tone became fierce. "You see this ring It has been the cause of all my unutter-

able woe. You!" he continued must never know my history.
I would not wring the heart of 1 of my countrymen for all
the riches in Italy Take this ring said he & keep it in re-
membrance of me & should any outlaws of the mountains
ever attempt to rob you, show him this ring & he will
trouble you no farther for I am their king as he said this
he gave me the flashing jewell from off his finger take it
said he & when you look upon it remember Guilermore the
Bandit King Since then I have traveled many times through
Italy & this ring was law wherever I went

Harris

Among the essays which he wrote or began to write in
the old book were "Sermons to Boys without a text, by
Marlowe," "Stability of Character" and "The Ruins of
Time," which gave him so much trouble that though he
sat down to it at least six times, he could never get more
than twenty-three lines written. Then there was an imaginary debate on the comparative mental capacity of man
and woman, wherein his admiration of his mother is seen
in his eloquent defense of woman's intellectual ability.
A part of it read:

Mr. Chairman: The question which is under the consideration of this able and distinguished body is whether or
not man is an intellectual superior of woman. I contend that
he is not, by any means, or else why does he unbosom his
trials and troubles to his wife and mother? . . . Look at the
mother of Washington—would he ever have been the great
scholar and noble General that he was if she had had no
intellect? Never! He would maybe have ended his life on
the gallows or in the penitentiary if his mother had never
had any intellect. What would become of man if it were

not for woman? How many rash acts has she kept him from doing? . . .

And in conclusion, the debator says, "I now bid you all Adieu and retire from public life."

Joel became an eager reader of newspapers, too. Eatonton was such a slow, sleepy little town that it hadn't a paper of its own, but Joel was always at the post office on the day when weekly papers came in from Milledgeville, which was then still the capital of Georgia, although Atlanta had now grown to be the larger city.

That post office at Eatonton was one of the queerest ever seen. It was in the basement of a little grocery store, with a part of the grocery stock all around it. The grocer and the postmaster were one and the same man—a Mr. Sidney Prudden, who had come down from Connecticut to Georgia so many years before that he had become almost as Southern as the Georgians—though most folk still thought of him as a "Yankee." His daughter Louise and Joel, when they were little children, had often studied from the same book in school.

The post office, just a desk and a few pigeonhole boxes, was in a corner of the room with a wooden and wire screen in front of it. Opposite it was an old sofa, upholstered in green. One of the back legs was broken, so that it tilted, leaning back against the wall for support. It was a very tired old sofa. Its springs groaned and creaked in protest when you sat down on it, and some of them were beginning to punch their way through the green upholstery. All around it were boxes and barrels on which patrons sat to read their mail and newspapers when there wasn't room enough on the sofa.

"War has begun! Our batteries are firing on the Yankees in Fort Sumter."

All other affairs were for the moment forgotten. Crowds gathered to discuss the event excitedly.

By the time he was twelve, Joel was sure to be there when the big mail bag brought by the stagecoach was opened. It brought, among other things, the *Recorder* and the *Federal Union,* the two weekly papers published in Milledgeville. These papers had many subscribers in Putnam County, so many in and around Eatonton that the postmaster would just stack them on a long shelf outside the post-office window, and while he was busy weighing sugar or selling an ax, each subscriber would pick out his own paper by the address.

One day when he was barely twelve, Joel said to Mr. Prudden, "May I read one of these papers, sir?"

"Certainly, Joel," replied the kindly postmaster. He had already noticed how longingly the boy looked at the papers. "Now, let's see—" He thumbed over them. "Here's one directed to Mr. Will Spivey. He lives out in the country and almost never comes in for it until Saturday. But be careful not to tear it or get it dirty."

"I will, sir," promised Joel. Thereafter, sitting on the old sofa or on a box, he read those papers so absorbedly that he often forgot where he was. The Civil War was just going into its second year, and the papers were full of war and political news and bitter editorials against the "Yankees." There would be bits of European news, jokes and poems, all of which Joel read with deep interest. The air around him was thick with the smells of cheese and camphine and salt fish and many other odorous things, but he said in after years that it had seemed to him the pleasantest place in the world. How he longed to be sitting at a desk in an editorial office—he noticed that the editors called it a "sanctum"—writing stuff like this!

CHAPTER FOUR

Joel Answers a "Want Ad"

JOEL never forgot that April day when the stage came
dashing in from Milledgeville, at higher speed than
usual, and the driver shouted, even before he reined
up in front of the post office:

"War has begun! Our batteries in Charleston harbor are
firing on the Yankees in Fort Sumter."

Those words were echoing in every town and hamlet
in the nation, and in Eatonton as elsewhere, all other affairs
were, for the moment, almost forgotten. Crowds gathered
to discuss the event excitedly. Some breathed defiance to
other Americans who had now become "the Enemy."
Many in the South were stricken with sadness at the
thought of separation from the Union, which had long
held their love and loyalty. Most of the young men, however, took fire in behalf of the South and began to ask
where they could join the fighting forces.

Mr. Leverette and Mrs. Harris were agreed upon the
doctrine that the Southern states had a right to secede from
the Union if they wished.

"But they won't be allowed to do it so easily," Mrs.
Harris insisted.

41

"Oh, there may be some little trouble," admitted Mr. Leverette, "but the Yankees in general won't fight. They're a lot of shopkeepers."

"I wish I could believe that," said Mrs. Harris slowly, "but I'm afraid you'll find we're in for a long spell of trouble." Her glance wandered to Joel, listening, open-mouthed, in a corner. He could not know at the moment what she was thinking, though the others guessed it from her next words.

"I wish the politicians who stir up these wars had to go into the armies!" she exclaimed bitterly. "I'm like the girl in the song, 'Jeannette and Jeannot':

> " 'Let those who make the quarrels
> Be the only ones to fight.' "

Rapidly the news came—"Virginia has left the Union and joined the Southern Confederacy." "Arkansas has joined!" "Tennessee!" "North Carolina." A company of volunteers, mostly young men, was raised at Eatonton and marched away amid tears and cheers and flag waving. Mr. Demetrios offered his service to the South, was accepted because of his previous military experience, and bade his friends in the little town farewell.

At first the fighting was hundreds of miles away from Putnam County, and as reports came back that the Southern troops were always victorious, the folks around Eatonton took things rather easily. Joel, however, began to be restless on his own account. When he reached his thirteenth birthday, he said to his mother, "I wish I could get a job." He had had little chance to earn any money. He found a chore to do now and then, such as running an errand, hoe-

"I don't like to see you working so hard, Mother," Joel said,
"while I am doing so little."

ing a neighbor's garden, or cutting or pulling weeds, but truth to tell, there were plenty of Negroes to do most of this work, and a small white boy had not much opportunity. He often wished that Eatonton had a newspaper, for he thought it would be fun to work in a newspaper office. When he read a paper, he did it over and over again, unconsciously studying the writing, imagining himself as having written it.

"I want you to go to school whenever you can, son," said his mother, as her needle flew into and out of a seam. "If you have an education, you can get a much better position."

"But I don't like to see you working so hard, Mother," said Joel, "while I'm doing so little."

She thrust her needle into the shirt she was making, drew him to her, and gave him a kiss. "Don't worry about that, honey," she said. "You help me a lot around the house, and you're doing most of the garden work now. Something will come up soon, I am sure."

But no opening appeared for him that winter. And now the war was beginning its second year, and both sides, each of which had thought it would be over in three months, were beginning to realize that the thing was more serious than they had expected. Calls for more men were sent out by both governments.

"You were right, Mrs. Harris," sighed Mr. Leverette, when a second volunteer company was being organized in Eatonton. "I'm afraid we are in for a long and terrible ordeal."

This second company was sent away to join the Southern armies in Virginia. Meanwhile, other men had gone from Eatonton to Augusta or Milledgeville and had joined other new groups of volunteers. The young man in good health and not crippled who was still at home was apt to hear someone in his vicinity crooning a line from the popular song, "Captain Jinks":

> " 'Mamma,' she cried,
> 'He ain't cut out for the ar-my.' "

Joel noticed that the grown-up people who came to the store and post office were now mostly women and old men. The war was taking heavy toll from Putnam County, as from everywhere else. There were no young men left in Eatonton, and even many of the middle-aged ones who used to smile at him and say "Howdy, Joel!" or "Hello, Tinktum!" were gone. He noticed, too, that after news of a battle had arrived, the women and girls came every day and lingered wistfully about the post office, hoping yet dreading to hear something about someone they loved.

One cold February day, just after the mail coach had passed, Joel heard the postmaster say to Mr. Anderson, an elderly lawyer of the town, "Here's a copy of a telegram that came to Madison this morning. The stage driver just brought it over. Not very pleasant news."

There were quite a number of people in the store, and two or three who overheard this said at once, "What is it?" "What's the news?" Mr. Anderson looked the paper over slowly and finally said, "I'll read it aloud." He mounted a small box and read:

> "Fort Donelson surrendered by General Buckner to Northern General Grant. Two thousand lost in battle and probably ten thousand taken prisoners. Generals Floyd and Pillow escaped before the surrender with probably four thousand men."

Mr. Anderson's voice shook a little as he read. There was a dead silence for a moment after he had concluded; then another elderly man sighed and said, "That's a serious blow to us. That Yankee general is liable to come right on up the Tennessee River now, into Alabama and Georgia."

"Never!" exclaimed another. "Albert Sidney Johnston will stop him."

"General Johnston has been begging all winter for more soldiers," said Mr. Anderson. "There must be more recruiting if we are to stop them. They have us outnumbered."

Joel's blood chilled at the thought that Georgia might be invaded. It was sad, too, to see, shortly after this, boys only three or four years older than himself enlisting and being sent northward to the battlefields. He saw his mother looking at him sometimes with frightened eyes, and now he guessed what she was thinking. He had been thinking of it, too: That perhaps the time would come when he would be old enough and big enough to shoulder a gun like the rest of them and march away to war—and maybe never come back. Then his mother would be one of those women who went daily to the post office, hoping and dreading, until the awful news came.

But only a few days after the reading of that telegram which brought such ill tidings, Joel's eye fell upon a paragraph in a Milledgeville paper, which sent his thoughts into an exciting new channel. It was an advertisement signed by Mr. Turner, the planter for whose family his mother had done some sewing. It announced that on the following Tuesday, March 4th, the undersigned would publish the first number of *The Countryman,* a weekly paper, at his home, Turnwold, northeast of Eatonton.

Turner announced that the new publication would be modeled after Mr. Addison's little paper, *The Spectator,* Mr. Goldsmith's little paper, *The Bee,* and Dr. Johnson's little paper, *The Rambler*—all eighteenth-century leaflets consisting entirely of essays. Joel had never read any of these things, though he had frequently seen quotations from them and references to them in the papers and magazines.

He could scarcely wait until the following Tuesday to see what *The Countryman* would be like. It had just as many pages as the Milledgeville papers—four—but its pages were smaller. Joel devoured every word of it, from beginning to end, and thought it the most interesting paper he had ever seen. Perhaps his judgment was influenced by one column which was headed "Advertisements." The first paragraph in this column read:

> The Countryman is published every Tuesday morning upon the plantation of the editor, away off in the country, 9 miles from any town or village.

A little way below this was another paragraph which brought Joel's heart into his mouth:

> An active, intelligent white boy, 14 or 15 years of age, is wanted at this office, to learn the printing business. March 4th, 1862.

Joel read it a second and a third time. Was this the answer to all his hopes? He ran all the way home and burst into the house excitedly.

"Oh, Mother, Mr. J. A. Turner has started a newspaper,

and he wants a boy to learn the printing trade. May I write to him and see if he will take me?"

His mother felt herself grow cold all over. She laid down her sewing and looked at him, trying to keep her sorrow from appearing in her face. The moment that she had so long dreaded had come—when her only child would leave home to begin his life work, and perhaps never live with her again.

"Would he want you to go out to Turnwold to stay?" she asked.

"Why, yes, I guess so. The newspaper's printed there."

"You want to go very much, don't you, honey?" she asked, struggling with her feelings.

"Why, yes, Mother, the newspaper business is just what I want to get into. I want to write things myself. I'll be awfully sorry to leave you, but you'll have Grandma here with you, and I'll come back and see you as often as I can, and when I begin earning enough money, I'm going to have you come and live with me."

She gave him a hug and wiped away some tears. "Yes, dear, you may write to Mr. Turner. You seem awfully young to go into business. Didn't he say in his advertisement how old the boy must be?"

Joel looked a bit uneasy. "Well, the notice said fourteen or fifteen," he admitted, "but it won't be long until I'm fourteen."

"Only eight months." She smiled at him. "I'm afraid he will think you are too young. But write to him and see what he says."

"Is there a nice, clean sheet of writing paper in the cupboard?" he asked.

"Yes, but I think you'd better write your letter first on

brown paper, and then you can make changes in it, if you like, before you copy it. Be careful with your spelling."

He wrote out his letter on the brown paper with the little piece of lead pencil which they owned—and even that must be preserved very carefully, for pencils cost ten or fifteen cents apiece then. He crossed out parts of the letter and rewrote, and crossed out again. Finally he said, "Do you think this will do?" and read it aloud.

"Yes, I think that will be all right," his mother replied. She wanted it to be all his own composition, so she made no suggestion. But she thought it best to look it over. "You have left the 't' out of respectfully," she pointed out.

"Oh yes," exclaimed Joel, correcting it hastily.

"If you're going to be a printer, you mustn't make mistakes in spelling," she reminded him.

"Yes ma'am, I know that," he admitted. "I left that out because I was in such a hurry." He was becoming a much better speller in the past year or so.

Now he carefully cleaned the point of their only pen, dipped it into the home-made ink, and wrote:

Mr. J. A. Turner,
Turnwold Plantation,
Putnam County, Ga.

My Dear Sir:

I saw your notice in the Countryman which said that you wanted a boy to learn the printing trade. I should like to have the place, for I have always wanted to work in a newspaper office. I am not fourteen yet, but I will be in December. My mother is poor, and I must earn some money very soon. I have gone to school and to the academy, and have studied grammar, spelling, geography, reading and arithmetic. I would promise to work very hard and do what is right.

Yours very respectfully,

JOEL C. HARRIS

He hurried to the post office, mailed the letter, and thought about little else for days afterward. A week passed and he heard nothing.

"Now that Mr. William Turner has gone with the army," said Mrs. Harris, "I wonder if their law office here in town is still kept open."

"Mr. J. A. is supposed to be in the office for a while on Tuesdays and Saturdays," replied Joel, "but sometimes when the weather is very bad, he doesn't come in. I haven't seen him this week."

Then came the next number of *The Countryman* to the post office, and Joel scanned it eagerly. There was the advertisement for the boy again, exactly as it had been the week before. His heart sank, and he went home more doleful than he had ever been in his life.

"I suppose he thinks I'm not old enough," he told his mother.

"I was afraid of that, dear," she replied.

But they had guessed wrongly. On Saturday forenoon there came a businesslike rap upon their door, and when Joel's mother opened it, there stood a stalwart, efficient-looking man with a fine, intelligent face—Mr. Turner himself.

"Why, how do you do, Mr. Turner!" exclaimed Mrs. Harris, her nerves in a flutter, for she guessed his errand. "Come in and sit down."

"Your boy wrote me a letter," Mr. Turner said when

they were seated, "asking for a place as apprentice to the printing trade." He took the letter from his pocket.

"Yes sir, I know about it," said Mrs. Harris.

"And you are willing for him to go into the business?"

"I suppose I must be willing," she replied. "He's all I have, but we are poor, and he is so eager to go to work, especially in the printing business—I think he prefers that above anything else—that I must let him go."

"I suppose you understand, Mrs. Harris," said Mr. Turner, "that an apprentice receives no wages. I can give him only board and clothing, but I shall see to it that both are of good quality."

"Perhaps better than he gets at home." His mother smiled a bit sadly.

"As soon as he learns his trade, I can begin to pay him a small wage," Mr. Turner went on.

"There is one thing I must say," Mrs. Harris interposed, looking bravely into Mr. Turner's eyes, for she was a woman of spirit. "Joel is my only child, and I must know that he is not living with anyone who will be a bad influence on him. I would want him to live in your own house."

This was a rather startling demand to be made in behalf of a poor boy seeking a place as apprentice. Mr. Turner pulled his mustache thoughtfully, and after a moment's hesitation, said:

"Well, that can probably be arranged, Mrs. Harris. I don't mind telling you that I want your boy. I have asked his teachers about him, and I hear that he is one of the brightest lads in school. Perhaps it can be arranged."

"It must be so," she said firmly. "It is the only condition upon which I can let him go."

"All right, I will make it a promise," he agreed. "For

the first few nights, I may have to put him to sleep at the home of my printer, Mr. Wilson. But Wilson's a good fellow, and as soon as we can get a room ready, I'll take Joel into my house. Is he at home? I'd like to speak to him."

"Yes sir, he is in the garden. We are just planting our Irish potatoes. I'll call him."

She did not tell Joel what was wanted, and he came in, all unsuspecting. When he saw Mr. Turner, his breath almost left him for a moment, and his face flushed rosy red, all the way around to the back of his neck. Even when he became an old man, it did that when he was asked to meet admiring strangers or when he was praised in public. He never got over his boyhood shyness.

But Mr. Turner tried to put him at his ease. With a friendly smile, he courteously arose to shake hands with the boy, just as if he had been a man, a piece of kindliness and a lesson in politeness which Joel never forgot.

"Did you write all this letter yourself, Joel?" asked Mr. Turner, tapping it with his finger.

"Y-yes s-sir," replied Joel. To save his life, he couldn't help stuttering a little in moments of excitement.

"And so you'd like to be a printer?"

"Y-yes sir," said Joel. "A printer at first, and then a writer—or editor."

Mr. Turner smiled at him, but kindly. "I'm glad to see that you have ambition," he said. "You're smaller and younger than I had expected my apprentice to be, but I hear that you do very well at school, and if my business is what you would like to go into, why, you're apt to do pretty well with that, too. How soon could you come out to Turnwold?"

"Any time," answered Joel.

"Today?"

"Yes sir." Joel looked at his mother, and when he saw how her hands were trembling, how she was striving to hold back the tears, he began to realize fully for the first time what this step meant, and feared that his readiness to go must seem rather cruel to her.

"He will be only nine miles away from you," said Mr. Turner, understanding her emotion. "I'll bring him or send him in to see you every now and then. It isn't as if I were taking him away off somewhere, into another state. Could you be ready in two hours?" he said, turning to Joel.

"Yes sir." Joel knew that he could be ready much sooner than that. He had so little to pack.

"My man Harbert will be coming in with a wagon in a day or two," said Mr. Turner. "He will bring your trunk out."

When Mr. Turner was gone, Joel's mother told him to bring out from a closet a tiny trunk, only slightly larger than a modern suitcase, and in it she put his extra shirts, some socks, and his working clothes, for he was now dressing himself in his Sunday suit, already growing shiny at the seams, for the drive to the country.

"Where are your marbles and ball?" asked his grandmother.

"I'm not going to take them," replied Joel stoutly. "I won't have time to play with them now, Grandma. I'll have to work." He had the feeling that he was putting his boyhood behind him. He could not foresee that he would have much time for play at Turnwold.

He still had fears that his luck was too good to last. "Mother," said he, "suppose Mr. Turner is drafted into the army?"

"He won't be," she replied confidently. "He is slightly lame, because of a childhood illness, and he is too valuable where he is. He is really worth a whole company of soldiers to our government. He is producing large quantities of food on his plantation, and he has some other industries there, too, you know—a tannery, a hat factory, a distillery, not to mention the printing office. Think how much leather the armies need for shoes, saddles, harness, and other things. Without men like Mr. Turner here at home, our soldiers could not fight."

Grandmother went over and told the Leverettes of Joel's good fortune. Another neighbor, curious to know what was going on, came in to learn the reason for Mr. Turner's call and went out again to spread the news. Very soon it was all over town—Joel Harris was going to the big plantation to learn to be a printer.

All too soon Mr. Turner's buggy, drawn by a big handsome gray horse, came dashing up to the gate. Joel's mother clutched him tightly and kissed him again and again.

"G-good-by, Grandma. G-good-by, Mother," Joel said, trying to keep his own voice steady. "I'll come back for you someday."

CHAPTER FIVE

The New Employer

A S HE rode away, his mother stood at the gate, waving at him and trying to smile through her tears. Grandma waved one arm and kept the other comfortingly around her daughter. Joel was sorry that he had not time to say good-by to the postmaster and Uncle Bob Capers and other friends. But as they went down the street, they passed a group of his playmates, busy at a marble game.

"Good-by!" called Joel to them.

"Good-by! Good-by!" they cried, waving their hands. They had heard where he was going. Wistfully, Joel looked back at them and saw that their heads were again bent over their marble game. It hurt his feelings a little. He thought they should have grieved more at his departure. He had yet to learn that people's own affairs are most important of all to them. He now discovered, too, how sad a thing it is to leave home. All his life he was a lover of home and his family, and he was never quite happy when he was away from them.

Mr. Turner, who was a sympathetic and observant man, saw how depressed the boy was, and tried to enliven him by talking about the things they saw along the way, about trees and birds, which were favorite subjects with him. Presently he pointed out a log cabin by the roadside.

"That is where the high sheriff of our county lives," said he. "Do you know him—Colonel John B. Stith?"

"Yes sir," replied Joel, "but I thought he lived in a big, fine house. I don't see how he can get in at that door yonder."

"Why not?" asked Mr. Turner in surprise.

"The way he goes on," replied Joel. "I thought he'd be too big for that door. He is always in town talking politics, and he talks bigger than anybody."

Mr. Turner shouted with laughter. "Well, that is his house," said he. "When you're a little older, you will find many people more disappointing than the high sheriff. I've heard of boys being too big for their breeches, but this is the first time I've ever heard that a man could be too big for his house. That's a good one on the colonel."

He laughed again, and out of the corner of his eye he scanned Joel with a new interest. Evidently there was more to this homely, red-haired, bashful kid than one saw on the surface. He was a keen observer, and he had a sense of humor. "He'll make a fine reporter, perhaps a great editor someday," thought Mr. Turner.

But after that, Joel seemed to relapse into his loneliness again, and Mr. Turner said, "Can you drive a horse?"

"Yes sir," replied Joel quickly.

"Would you like to drive Ben Bolt a while?"

"Yes indeed," said Joel. He took the reins, glad to handle such a handsome, spirited animal, finer than any he had seen at the livery stable. But the big gray, immediately

*Joel took the reins, glad to handle such a handsome,
spirited animal.*

feeling a new and unfamiliar hand on the reins, tried to live up to his name by bolting. At high speed he galloped along the road, and had it not been almost straight and not very rough, there would have been danger of an accident. But Joel's slender arms were wiry, and he had had enough experience to know what to do in such a situation. Furthermore, he was one of those rare persons who seem to have a close understanding of animals and an unusual knack of controlling them. Mr. Turner, who was familiar with Ben Bolt's tricks, saw that the boy knew what he was about, so he said nothing and did nothing to interfere. After about a quarter of a mile of this wild dash, Joel got the horse slowed down to a trot again.

"You did that very well," said Mr. Turner. "I didn't know that little boys in town could drive horses."

"Oh, some of them can," replied Joel. "I've driven the livery stable horses and some others. If Ben Bolt had been really scared, I think I would have been scared myself, but he was only playing. He has been tied to the hitch rack a long time, and he must be getting hungry."

"Yes, he is," said Mr. Turner, and he went on talking about Ben Bolt and Rob Roy, his teammate, speaking of them almost as if they were human. Joel often thought of animals in that way himself, especially since hearing Uncle Bob Caper's stories, and it pleased him to think that he had ideas in common with a grown man, especially such a man as Mr. Turner.

"But you think you'd rather go into the publishing business than work with horses?" asked Mr. Turner after a while.

"Oh, I'd much rather!" exclaimed Joel.

"You like to read?"

"Yes sir, but I can never get hold of enough things to read."

"I'll see that you are supplied." Joel found himself liking this big, thoughtful man more and more every minute.

"We Turners are a reading family," the publisher remarked. "You might guess that from my name. My father christened me Joseph Addison, in honor of one of the greatest essayists in English literature. Addison wrote poems and plays, too, but he and a man named Steele wrote a series of essays in a little paper they called *The Spectator* and another called *The Tatler,* which— Well, that was a hundred and fifty years ago, and nobody has ever been able to equal them since. Have you read any of them?"

"No sir, but I've heard of them."

"You must read them sometime. I have them and many other books. My father had a library of four thousand volumes."

"My goodness!" exclaimed Joel. His brain was staggered by the thought of so many books in a private home. What happy hours he could spend in such a place!

"It was in the old family mansion, not far from where I live," Mr. Turner went on. "You shall see it someday soon. My older brother William lives there now. When my father died and the estate was divided, William and I took most of the books. I've bought many since, so I now have about two thousand volumes. William is even more literary than I am; that is, he doesn't pay as much attention to farming as I do, and he has written a novel; got it published, too—first in a magazine, and then in book form."

"Is it a good story?" asked Joel.

Mr. Turner pursed his mouth in a funny little way. "Well, it's in good taste and the English is excellent," he said, "but I don't think Dickens and Thackeray will need to worry about their laurels. But don't you tell Mr. William that I said that," he added, turning on Joel suddenly. "I'll skin you alive if you do."

Joel laughed heartily at the mock threat.

"I've written everything imaginable myself," Mr. Turner continued, "even short stories. A young fellow sometimes tries several things before he finds out what he wants. I've always wanted to do something with books. I taught school for a year when I was a very young man. Then I studied law and I've practiced at it, off and on, ever since. But to be honest with you, Joe, I think lawyers are a nuisance."

Joel saw that he was going to enjoy his friendship with this humorous, original man.

"I mean it!" affirmed Mr. Turner. "One trouble with the South is that too many of our brightest men have gone into politics, instead of producing something. That is one thing that helped me to decide that I ought to settle down here on the land. When my father died, I could not endure the thought of seeing this big, fertile plantation passing out of the family or being allowed to go to rack and ruin. So here I am—but still tinkering with literature. You probably don't know that this is the fifth time I have tried to be a publisher."

"No sir."

"It's a fact. Fourteen years ago—I was much younger then, you see, and hadn't the experience that I have now— I started a magazine which I called *Turner's Monthly,* and issued just three numbers of it."

"Why didn't you print any more?" Joel wondered.

"Because people just wouldn't read the thing," replied Mr. Turner, so solemnly that Joel smiled in spite of himself, "and it seemed to me that a publisher must sell a few copies of a magazine if he wanted to keep going. The second one I tried turned out still worse. I issued just one number! Then I tried a weekly, the *Independent Press,* while I was practicing law regularly in Eatonton, but I was too busy with the law to keep it going.

"Two years ago, I launched another magazine, a quarterly called *The Plantation,* just to defend our slavery system against Northern attack upon it. Then the war came on and made this unnecessary, so I dropped it. Now I believe I have started a sheet which has a better chance to survive than any of the others. Don't you think so?"

"Oh yes, I do!" exclaimed Joel. "I think it's the most interesting paper I have ever seen." His enthusiasm was so genuine that Mr. Turner could not but be gratified.

The sun had set, a ball of fire among dark, red-edged clouds, and darkness fell quickly, as it does in the South. The heavy clouds rolled up and covered the stars, so that Joel could no longer see the road.

"I can't see where I am going," he said, "and if the road forks, I wouldn't know it."

"Don't worry about that," advised Mr. Turner. "Just let Ben have his way. He can see in the darkness when we can't, and he knows the road home even better than I do."

It grew much colder, and Joel hoped they would reach Turnwold soon. Ben Bolt trotted on confidently. Presently he slowed up to a walk, and they went down a steep slope. Joel could see that there were forests on each side, and the darkness was blacker than ever. Suddenly Ben was splashing through water, and the buggy was bouncing over large pebbles on the bed of a stream.

"This is Crooked Creek," said Mr. Turner. "When you

see it by daylight, you will know how it got its name."

Ben climbed another grade on the other side of the creek, reached level ground, and broke into a trot again, this time faster than before.

"Level road now, and on the home stretch," said Mr. Turner. "He is thinking of that comfortable stall and his supper.

"For three or four days," he said, after a pause, "I am going to let you sleep and board with Mr. and Mrs. Wilson. Mr. Wilson is my printer; has charge of the shop where you will work, and lives near it. He is an Irishman and a quaint character; an amateur actor—or thinks he is. He'll spout Shakespeare at you by the hour, if you'll let him. Pretty good singer, too. Mrs. Wilson is a fine housekeeper, and I think you will be comfortable there, and have a good time, too."

Ben again slowed his pace to a walk, turned aside and stopped. Joel could just dimly see a gap in the trees in front of him. Someone was evidently awaiting their arrival, for he heard the clank of a chain, and then the creak of a big gate being opened.

"Is that you, Harbert?" called Mr. Turner.

"Yas, Marster," answered a Negro's voice.

"As soon as we get to the house," said Mr. Turner, as Ben started walking through the gate without waiting for instructions, "I want you to take Mr. Harris here over to Mr. Wilson's place."

"Yassir."

"Welcome to Turnwold, Joel," said the planter as he climbed out of the buggy. "I hope the Wilsons will make things comfortable for you, and I think they will. Good night."

"Good night, sir."

The old Negro climbed into the buggy in Mr. Turner's place and took the reins. Joel could not imagine how they found their way in the darkness, but they went through another gate and apparently along a lane and among some trees until they saw a light gleaming from a window. As they drew up in front of the house, Harbert, in the musical voice which seems to be a peculiar gift of the colored race, called out, "Hello!" (This is the old-time way of announcing your arrival by vehicle in the country.)

Instantly there was a muffled reply from inside the cottage, the door was flung open, and a man came striding out.

"Ah, and it's the young man," said Mr. Wilson, for this was he. "Jump right down, Mr. Harris, and come in to the warmth of the fire. Have you any baggage?"

"I's gittin' it, Mr. Wilson," said Harbert. "I'll bring it in."

The bulky figure of a woman was now framed in the light of the doorway. "Come on in, lad," said her motherly voice. "I've got your supper ready and kept hot on the hearth for ye."

Joel, though warmed by the kindliness of their welcome, yet stumbled into the house, blushing and ill at ease, as he always was in the presence of strangers. And thus he entered into what was for him a new world.

CHAPTER SIX

The Young Printer

NOW, when a man goes into the printing business," said Mr. Wilson next morning, as they entered the little wooden building where *The Countryman* was published, "he usually starts as the divil. D'ye know what that means?"

"I don't believe I do," said Joel.

"Well, the divil is the feller who washes the type after it's been used, and does chores around the shop. But don't feel bad about that. We'll have you setting type before long. I had old Aunt Dilsey make ye an apron yesterday, for printer's ink is sticky stuff, ye see, and ye can't afford to get it on yer clothes. Let's put it on."

He hung the loop over Joel's head, tied the waist strings behind him, and stepped back with his hand at his chin to survey the result. The apron came down almost to Joel's toes.

"We didn't think ye would be quite so—so young," said Mr. Wilson, apologetically, "and so she made it a wee bit long. But no matter, it isn't quite long enough for ye to step on, anyhow. I'll have it shortened tonight.

"Now, here on this stone table," he continued, leading

the way to it, "lies the type from which this week's *Countryman* was printed. Ye see, it's in what we call a form. The first thing for ye to do is to wash the ink off it with this solution of lye and water. I'll show ye how to mix the stuff later. Then we'll be ready to distribute the type back in the cases."

It must be remembered that in those days there were no typesetting machines as there are now. All type for printing must be set by hand; each tiny letter picked out of a series of little boxes and set in line.

Joel looked at the black, dingy mass of metal and was thrilled to think that this had created the interesting paper which he had read only two or three days ago. Even the pungent odor of the ink was fascinating. Slowly he read two or three of the remembered sentences; slowly, because he must read upside down, from left to right, instead of in the usual way. From that moment to the end of his life, the smell of printer's ink was always a homelike and pleasant fragrance to him, as it is to all real newspapermen.

He began to wash the type, while Mr. Wilson, busy at something else, sang in a powerful baritone voice:

"Believe me, if all those endearing young charms
  Which I gaze on so fondly to-day,
Were to change by to-morrow, and fleet in my arms
  Like fairy gifts fading away. . . ."

He made his voice quiver mournfully in the pathetic passages.

"Ah, Tom Moore's the gr-rand poet," he exclaimed, when he had completed the song. "Have ye ever read his writings, Joel?"

"No sir," said Joel. "Is he the one who wrote that song, 'Come Ye Disconsolate,' that they sing in church sometimes? I notice the hymn book says it's by Thomas Moore."

"The very one!" affirmed Mr. Wilson.

"I think that's a beautiful song,' 'said Joel.

"No finer ever written," agreed Mr. Wilson. "Ye must read all his poems, me boy. Your education isn't complete wit'out them. Now you'd better bring in an armful of wood and chunk that fire a bit."

"A part of your job," he went on, when Joel had brought the wood and put two sticks of it into the sheet-iron stove, "will be to bring wood, keep up the fire, clean the ashes out of the stove ivery day or two and sweep the floor—well, say, two or three times a week. Of course, sweeping the floor is jist putting on airs, for nobody but women iver ixpects a print shop to be clean. But me wife or Mrs. Turner is liable to drop in once in a while, and the mere contimptuous way they look about the place is enough to make a man's flesh creep. So we'll have to sweep out now and thin, jist for the sake of our peace of mind.

"Now, I'll show ye how to distribute," he said, when the type was fairly dry. "Here's a box for ye to stand on. See this big tray—we call it a case—all partitioned off in little square boxes? Well, each one of those little squares contains a letter or figure. This one has all the *a's* in it, this one all the *b's* . . ." And so he went on, all through the alphabet. "And here are the figures—*1, 2, 3* . . ." he went on, touching the compartments with his fingertip. "And this case up above the other contains the capital letters—*A, B, C, D,* and so on. You see why we printers always call the small letters 'lower case.' My, my! It's a long reach

"A part of your job," he said, "will be to keep the fire going."

for ye up to that upper case. I'll have to get ye a bigger box to stand on."

He searched for one and dropped it before the cases. "Now, look at ivery letter carefully," he directed, "before you throw it into the case. Miny of the errors in print are made because the type is badly distributed, and whin the printer goes to set type again and reaches into the *a* box, he gets a *q* instid. Ye know what the immortal Shakespeare said of errors: 'O, hateful Error, Melancholy's child!' And there niver was a truer word spoken."

Joel soon became deeply interested in the task of distribution, and did very well with it. In an hour or so, Mr. Turner dropped in, asking genially, "How is our young printer getting along?" and bringing several sheets of manuscript which he handed to Mr. Wilson. "For next week's paper," he said. He stayed a few minutes, talking to the two, then mounted his horse and rode out into the fields. Spring planting of crops was going on, and everybody was busy.

"There are a hundred and twenty slaves on the plantation," Mr. Wilson told Joel, "and those of thim who are not farmers or experts wit' cattle, horses, or hogs, know some other trade. There are tanners, carpenters, cobblers, blacksmiths, and masons. Many of the women can spin cotton and wool into thread and dye it, knit stockings, weave cloth and carpet, make clothes for the Negro men, women, and children, make butter and do a lot of other things."

They closed the shop at six o'clock and went home for supper. At the table, Mr. Wilson, who loved to talk, entertained Joel with a sketch of his own life, telling of his birth and boyhood in Belfast, a big manufacturing city in northern Ireland, how he was brought to America when he was a boy, and had been nearly all over the United States since then, sometimes actually as a tramp. He had learned the printer's trade in early youth, but a longing to go on the stage and a love of wandering kept him from working at his trade as he should have.

"I wint to California eleven years ago," he said. "That was jist after the first big wave of the Gold Rush, ye know. I rode part of the way on a wagon and walked part of the way over the Rocky Mountains. I worked in newspaper offices in San Francisco and the mining camps, and now and thin I acted in the theaters. I'd have ye know, young sir, that I acted out there wit' the great Junius Brutus Booth."

"As the Second Grave Digger in Hamlet," said Mrs. Wilson, winking at Joel.

"Woman, do not deceive the lad," exclaimed Mr. Wilson, "I played more important parts than that. I was Earl Rivers to his Richard the Third. Ye see," he explained to Joel, "whin a great actor like Booth travels around, especially to a far place like California, he takes no troupe of his own wit' him. There's a company of actors in the theaters in every big city to play all the lesser parts. At least, that used to be the case. They're beginning to take more actors with thim now whin they travel.

"Well, whin Booth left California, I was dissatisfied, and I followed him back to New Orleans. Worked me way on a ship down to Panama. They had jist got the railroad finished across the Isthmus then; before that time, ye had to ride across it on muleback or walk. Well, I got up to New Orleans on a tramp schooner, and Mr. Booth remimbered me. Yes sir, he remimbered me well." Mr. Wilson was pathetically proud of that. "But they had a good com-

pany of actors in New Orleans, and I could only get the
part of Seyton in Macbeth. But ah!" He shook his finger
in air at Joel. "As Seyton I gave him the cue for one of
the grandest speeches in all the immortal bard's works.
It's in the last act, d'ye mind, when the inemy troops are
approaching, and Macbeth is very near his end."

Mr. Wilson sprang up from the table, ran to a closet
and got his wife's mantilla, a sort of long cloak or cape,
tossed it over his back, brought one corner of it up across
his chest and threw it over his shoulder in the old tragic
style. Mrs. Wilson was protesting: "Pack of nonsense!"
But he paid no attention to her.

"Macbeth," Mr. Wilson said to Joel, "is alone in a room
of his palace when Seyton (that was me) comes in and
says, 'The queen, me lord, is dead.' At that, Booth, as Macbeth, seemed to turn to stone; you could jist feel him
growing cold. As if he hardly knew what he was saying,
he muttered—but that wonderful voice of his carried to
the very back seats:

> " 'She should have died hereafter;
>   There would have been a time for such a word.' "

Mr. Wilson's own voice deepened as he imitated the great
tragedian, and Joel listened with a growing fascination.

"Macbeth was beginning to see," Mr. Wilson went on,
"that his own doom was at hand; and wit' his eyes fixed
on distance he then utters that matchless soliloquy, one of
the greatest passages in all literature:

> " 'Tomorrow, and tomorrow, and tomorrow,
>   Creeps in this petty pace from day to day,

To the last syllable of recorded time;
And all our yesterdays have lighted fools
The way to dusty death. Out, out, brief candle!
Life's but a walking shadow, a poor player
That struts and frets his hour upon the stage
And then is heard no more; it is a tale
Told by an idiot, full of sound and fury,
Signifying nothing.' "

Joel felt his skin prickle, his nerves tingle to his finger-tips as he listened to these lines which the world has admired for three hundred years. He forgot Mr. Turner's joking remarks about Wilson's acting. The beauty and grandeur of the language, spoken not at all badly by this humble would-be actor, gave the boy for the first time an inkling of how wonderful a thing great drama may be when well presented on the stage.

"I felt as if I had a hand in that speech," said Mr. Wilson, putting the mantilla away and sitting down to eat his pie, "for he couldn't have spoken it if I hadn't told him the news about the queen. I hoped that I could act wit' Booth again, but he died on a Mississippi River steamboat, jist after leaving New Orleans. That was nine year ago last Novimber. Tom Moore had died only a few months before. It was a sad year for the arts."

He continued talking after supper, telling of his travels, while Joel eagerly drank in every word. The memories of this tramp printer and cheap actor, who nevertheless had an understanding of great thought and a love of beauty, opened for the boy the gates of another new world—that world outside his own little county, of which he had read much, but which these stories seemed to make ten times more real. But the evening was not all talk. Mr. Wilson sang "The Last Rose of Summer" and other ballads, the majority of them Irish, though among them was one beginning, "Who is Sylvia?"

"That is from *The Two Gintlemen of Verona*," he told Joel. "I was once one of the serenaders who sang it—in the Chatham Theatre in New York."

Finally, he took two books from a shelf. "These are some of Tom Moore's poems," said he, "but ye won't have time to read thim tonight, if we are to be up at half-past five in the morning. Another evening I won't talk ye to death; I'll let ye read a bit."

For the first few days, Joel was so busy with the task of learning the printer's trade that he had few idle moments. After he had distributed the type from this week's edition, Mr. Wilson said, "Now suppose ye learn composition— that's what we call typesetting, ye know. Let's see you set up this line, 'The Confederate States of America.' Here's what we call a stick—" And he handed Joel a metal holder which was just the width of a newspaper column and showed him how to place the type in it and how to put spaces between the words.

"Now, don't ask me any quistions," said he. "Jist pick out the type for yerself." And he went across the room and busied himself with something else.

Joel worked for twenty minutes, and finally said, "Here it is, Mr. Wilson."

The printer looked at the line of type, put it between two pieces of metal on the stone table, and tied a string around it all to hold it together. Then he lightly ran a roller covered with ink over the type, laid a piece of paper over it and took a proof of it. He showed the paper to

Joel, who blushed as red as a poppy when he saw it. This is the way it appeared:

The ConJedrate Staɹe sof america.

"Not bad for a first attimpt," said Mr. Wilson. "Ye need another *e* in Confederate, and letters ought to be right side up—"

"I know," said Joel, "but those tall letters fool me sometimes, and I clean forgot about that capital *A* in America. I'll do better next time."

He continued practicing until in a few days he could compose fairly well. Mr. Turner brought in more copy for the next week's issue, and by Friday morning they had the type all set for it. When the last letter was in place, the type locked up in the forms, Mr. Wilson began inking his roller to take proofs, and burst into song:

> "The harp that once through Tara's halls
>   The soul of music shed,
> Now hangs as mute on Tara's walls
>   As if that soul were fled. . . .

"Ah, there's nothing like a nice, sad song to sing when ye're happy!" he said, grinning at Joel. "Tom Moore, true Irishman that he was, the happiest of men, yet wrote a thousand sweetly sad poems. There's one that comes to me mind many a time, and means much to a rover like me. You'll begin to understand it, too, Joel, now that ye've left home. It starts like this." He paused, his right hand leaning on the roller handle, while he gestured with his left:

> "As slow our ship her foamy track
>   Against the wind was cleaving,

Her trimbling pinnant still looked back
To that dear Isle 'twas leaving.
So loth we part from all we love,
From all the links that bind us,
So turn our hearts as on we rove,
To those we've left behind us."

True enough, the recitation brought a lump into Joel's throat as he thought of his mother back there in Eatonton. The warm-hearted Irishman, seeing how near the tears were to his eyes, was seized with remorse.

"I didn't mane to make ye unhappy, me lad," he said. "Come, let's be gay!" He whistled a jig and did a little shuffle with his feet, bringing back a smile to his young helper's countenance.

Presently, Joel was sent over to the Turner residence with the proofs. It was the first time he had seen the place by daylight. It was just a big, plain, weatherboarded farmhouse, but it had an attractive setting. A row of tall, pointed cedars screened it from the main road, and in them mocking birds and other songsters nested. At some distance back of the house was a great, scattering grove of trees, among which were the Negro cabins—quite a village of them.

A pack of five rather small hounds, something like beagles, came galloping toward him, barking and woofing as he neared the house, but Joel, who understood dogs pretty well, soon saw that they were not vicious; in fact they were very good-natured—too much so, Mrs. Turner declared, to be worth their salt, though Mr. Turner strenuously denied this.

"They are harriers," Mr. Turner said to Joel. "We have

rabbit chases here sometimes, and you shall join in the fun with us when we do." He introduced Mrs. Turner and the children, some of whom had already come out to the printing shop and made friends with Joel.

"Tomorrow you move in here with us," said Mrs. Turner. "I'll show you your room."

It was a pleasant room on the second floor, so comfortably furnished that it seemed magnificent to poor Joel, who was not accustomed to such luxury.

On Monday the printing of *The Countryman* began.

"Our equipment is not of the best," complained Mr. Wilson to Joel. "The boss bought the whole outfit—type, press, cases and all—from a busted newspaper down the state somewhere. We are short of leads, and all the type foundries are in the North, so where are we to buy any? The boss is beggin' other publishers for some now."

He showed Joel a notice in the paper:

Will not some good brother printer sell me, as a special favor, a few pounds of leads, 18 em, long primer, 6 to pica? You can't tell how grateful such a favor would make me.

There was only a hand press, and this made the printing a laborious task. Most newspapers, however, were printed on hand-operated presses in those days. The form of type was laid on what was called the bed of the press, and the ink roller was passed across it until the type was well inked. Then a sheet of damp paper was laid over it, and it was slid under the platen, a large, flat metal plate which came down and pressed the paper against the type. To make it do this, the printer had to pull hard on a big wooden handle which stuck out from the press. This task required too much strength for Joel's small body, and Mr. Wilson had to do it—putting one foot against the wall when he pulled the lever, to get more pressure.

"Our subscription list is increasin' so fast," he told Joel, "that I must have help on this job before long."

Indeed, the people in Putnam County liked *The Countryman* so much that new subscriptions were coming in from them every week, and many from outside the county followed them. Presently Mr. Turner ordered a stalwart Negro named Cupid to come in each week and help work the press. Joel enjoyed having Cupid in the shop because of his funny remarks and because he rolled his eyes and grunted loudly every time he pulled the lever, pretending that the work was so much harder than it really was for him.

The paper eventually had a circulation of 2,000 copies, and was being read all over Georgia and even in the neighboring states. Before that point was reached, Mr. Turner had taken on a young man of the neighborhood named Jim Harrison—who played a large part in Joel's later life— and everybody, including the boss, had to work two days, far into the night, to get all the papers printed and addressed.

CHAPTER SEVEN

The First Time in Print

DESPITE the friendliness of those around him, Joel, far from his mother and from the friends who were all he had ever known, had his lonely hours for a while after going to Turnwold, and would have had more of them had there not been so much of interest to see and do on the great plantation, especially among its many kinds of wild life. As he worked, he heard squirrels scampering on the roof of the shop and blue jays cracking their acorns there. Once he looked up from his type case just in time to see a red fox cross the path leading into the woods, pause a moment with one forepaw in air to look toward the shop, and sniff the breeze, then vanish. As Joel remembered it in after years:

It was a great and saving experience. It was just lonely enough to bring me face to face with myself, and yet not lonely enough to breed melancholy. I used to sit in the dusk and see the shadows of all the great problems of life flitting about, restless and uneasy, and I had time to think about them. What some people call loneliness was to me a great blessing, and the printer's trade, so far as I learned it, was in the nature of a liberal education.

One of the most absorbing spectacles of that first spring was the building of a nest by a pair of partridges in last year's tall feed grass quite near the shop. Joel could not continue work for watching them until the job was complete.

First, they bent long grass over from each side until they made a tunnel three or four feet long. Then Mrs. Partridge went through it to the closed end and began to scratch and flutter, hollowing out a nest for herself. This disarranged the archway of grass, and Mr. Partridge rebuilt it carefully over her until she was completely concealed. Now and then he would walk away a few steps and look back at the nest. If his sharp eyes could see anything suspicious, he would return and weave the grass more closely together. Finally Mrs. Partridge came outside, they consulted over it with queer little cluckings, and decided that the job was well done. As Joel wrote of himself years later:

> Joe found it very difficult to discover the nest when he went out of the office, so deftly was it concealed; and he would have been compelled to hunt for it very carefully but for the fact that when Mrs. Partridge found herself disturbed, she rushed from the little grass tunnel and threw herself at Joe's feet, fluttering around as if desperately wounded, and uttering strange little cries of distress. Once she actually touched his feet with her wings; but when he stooped to pick her up, she managed to flutter off, just out of reach of his hand. Joe followed her for some distance, and he discovered that the farther she led him away from the nest, the more her condition improved, until finally, she ran off into the sedge and disappeared.

Joe was never able to find anyone to tell him how Mrs. Partridge knew what kind of antics a badly wounded bird would cut up.

Those first few evenings at Wilson's were lively, for the vivacious Irishman was either telling stories of his wanderings and his theatrical experiences, or throwing his wife's mantilla about him to recite Hamlet's soliloquy, or drawing his head down between his shoulders to snarl out Richard III's last rantings, or stuffing a pillow under his clothes to play Falstaff, or roaring out some ballad or other, so that Joel found it hard to steal an hour of quiet to read or to write to his mother. After he moved into the Turner home, his evenings were his own if he wanted them to be, and he was still so bashful in the presence of the family that he spent nearly all of them in his own room.

As he mastered his work at the shop, he found that except for the days when the paper went to press, he had many leisure hours when he might do just what he pleased, and those, when the weather was fine, he occupied in outdoor activities which became more and more varied—rambling through woods and fields, getting better acquainted with the wild things which lived among them, and—later—hunting, fishing, and trapping. He went over to look at the old Turner mansion, the former home of his employer's father, and lately the place where his bachelor brother William lived with his mother and widowed sister, Mrs. Hubert. The latter saw Joel walking in the grounds, and was very cordial.

"So this is young Mr. Harris," she exclaimed, shaking hands with the blushing boy. "I've been hearing of how fast you are learning the printing business. That's a fine little paper you are getting out over there, and I'm sure it will be a success."

She continued talking hospitably, showing Joel through the grounds. The handsome frame mansion, built in Colonial style, had a curving hedge of boxwood in front of it which scented the air. At one side was the family burying ground, enclosed by an iron fence. There were forests of splendid trees here, as at Turnwold, but Joel saw that Mr. William's farm was not as well kept as his brother's.

"My father was a great lover of trees," explained Mrs. Hubert. "He planted more trees than he cut down, and my brother Joseph is doing the same thing. That big grove of oaks and hickories between our two homes is the nesting place of many hawks, and the Negroes complain that they catch too many of our chickens. But as my brother says, you can grow a chicken in a few weeks, but it takes at least half a century to make a real tree, and of course he is right."

Joel found that Mr. Joseph Turner knew a great deal about forestry and botany; in fact, he loaned Joel books on those subjects and taught him much about them. Each spring he kept in a notebook the dates when he saw or heard the first migratory birds that came up from the South, and he would publish lists of these in *The Countryman,* as, for example:

Tues. 8th April.—Heard the first Martin (*hirundo purpurea*), also the first swallow (*hirundo pelasgia*).

Thurs. 10th. — Saw the first bee martin (*musicapa tyrannus*).

Wed. 16th.—Heard the first whippoorwill (*caprimulgus vociferus*).

And so on. Mrs. Turner was also a nature lover, and had a wonderful flower garden. She showed Joel through it, calling his attention especially to a large section which was devoted entirely to wild flowers. It is no wonder that he knew so much about nature through the rest of his life. He had a natural love for it, and he had teachers who made him love it the more.

When Joel brought the proofs of the paper to Mr. Turner each week, he was usually received in the library, which to him was the most wonderful thing on the plantation. The books almost covered three sides of a big room. It was easy to see how happy Mr. Turner was among them. During Joel's second or third visit, the editor took him on a tour of the shelves, pointing out the various authors.

"Here are *The Spectator* and *The Tatler,* which I told you about. Here are other eighteenth-century writers—Fielding, Swift, Smollett, Goldsmith.... Here are Gibbon's *Roman Empire,* histories of England by Macaulay and Hume . . . Irving, Fenimore Cooper's novels, Scott, Hugo . . . Dickens and Thackeray—but I haven't been able to get their very latest books, because of the war. Here are the poets—Shakespeare, Byron, Burns, Shelley, Keats, Wordsworth, Milton, Tasso; some American ones, too—Mr. Bryant, that New York editor; Professor Longfellow up at Harvard, who writes some very good things; a young Massachusetts Quaker named Whittier; our Southern poets, Paul Hamilton Hayne and Henry Timrod . . ."

Joel's eyes glistened at the sight of such a treasure house of reading, such an array of handsome volumes, for many of them were finely bound in leather, and some of them real book collectors' treasures.

"And here is our Southern novelist, William Gilmore

Simms, whom you ought to read," continued Mr. Turner.

"I've read most of his books," said Joel.

Mr. Turner, somewhat surprised, turned to the shelves again. "I'll lend you some books from time to time, if you'll take good care of them," said he.

"Oh, I certainly will do that, sir," exclaimed Joel.

"Now, let's see—" Mr. Turner looked along the shelves. "Here are Grimm's *Tales*—"

"I've read those," Joel told him.

"*Sandford and Merton*—"

"I've read that, too," said Joel. "Please, Mr. Turner, I'd like to have a volume of *The Spectator* or *Macbeth;* I've never read either of them."

His employer stared at him in surprise, then took two volumes from the shelves and handed them to him. "You may not understand it all," said he, "but I think you will get far more of it than most boys of your age."

After that, Joel was a frequent borrower from the library, with Mr. Turner either suggesting books for him to read or trying to give him what he wanted. He never ventured to go into the library alone. He was still too much in awe of the great collection and of Mr. Turner to go in and make himself at home there.

The fine mind concealed behind that freckle-faced, awkward, bashful exterior was evidently a source of wonder and interest to Mr. Turner, and he did everything he could to help Joel develop his talent. The young apprentice stole a march on him and secretly began displaying his ability before the employer realized it. This is how it happened:

The prospectus of *The Countryman,* as Mr. Turner wrote it, declared that

This paper is a complete cyclopedia of the History of the Times — The War News — Agriculture, stock-raising — Field-Sports — Wit — Humor — Anecdote — Tales — Philosophy — Morals — Poetry — Politics — Art — Science — Useful recipes — Money and Market Matters — Literature — Genl. Miscellany. . . .

This was a tremendous program for a small, four-page sheet, and Mr. Turner was being rather whimsical when he wrote it. He gave Joel a somewhat different picture.

"Of course, I can't pretend that this is a newspaper," he said. "On the other hand, we mustn't publish something that's dull and prosy. I just want it to be a pleasant and instructive companion for the leisure hour, a paper that will talk a little about something besides the war.

"But of course I can't ignore the war. I touch upon the political situation every week. My brother William writes a weekly letter from the front, and sometimes there are others. But I also try to write something of a literary sort every week, or publish a good poem.

"Much of our philosophy and wit must be handed out in very small packages—what we call fillers. You have noticed that the leading articles in newspapers cannot always be made to fit the space. There are little blank nooks at the bottom of the columns, which must be filled with short items or squibs of some sort or other. Most editors clip stuff from one another's papers to fill these crannies, but I like to give *The Countryman* a bit of a classical tone, so I have three books from which to lift short items. Here they are—*Lacon, The Percy Anecdotes,* and Rochefoucauld's *Maxims.*

"Now, I am going to give you the task of selecting next

week's fillers, and see how you get along with it. Count words and pick out something strong, brilliant, or interesting that will fill the space. You may have to prune it a little, but don't spoil a good sentence."

Joel enjoyed this new task greatly, finding much of interest in the three books through which he browsed. Mr. Turner sometimes criticized his selections, but for the most part was well satisfied. There might·be only one or two or three small fillers needed in a week's paper, but sometimes there was a space of a hundred words or so to be covered.

It wasn't long before Joel's mind began to itch with a desire to write something of his own for those spaces. He thought of so many things that he could say! Finally he jotted down several short items—comments upon events in history and literature—and one week when there was a space into which one of them would fit, he ventured to put it into type.

He watched Mr. Turner's face anxiously as he glanced over the proofs—now suddenly ridden by a fear that if he were found out, he might be discharged and sent back home. But the editor seemed to notice nothing wrong. Not until the paper was on the press did Joel breathe freely. How exciting it was to have fooled this wise man so completely! And next there came the supreme joy of seeing his own words in type for the first time—even though the readers of the paper did not know that they were his. In fact, Joel liked it better that way. For a long time after he began writing, he was so timid that he begged editors not to attach his name to anything they published.

More and more frequently he filled a space in *The Countryman* with a paragraph of his own, until at length he was drawing very little from the three books. He never wrote these items with pen or pencil—just composed them in type as he stood at the case. Thus no incriminating evidence was left lying around. He thought he was being very sly, and that Mr. Turner suspected nothing, but afterward he remembered a certain wise look which began to come to his employer's face, the hint of a smile about the corners of his mouth as he looked over the proofs—omens which should have signaled to the young scribe that he might have fooled the boss for a little while at the start, but he couldn't fool him long.

Only now and then was one of the fillers rejected. And what an honor it was to have one's writing in a paper which was admired by the best minds all over the South, and which was quoted from almost every week by other newspapers!

Joel had brought the old scrapbook with him to Turnwold, and continued to scribble in it—poems, stories, essays. He had now begun really to look forward to a literary career. "Just wait, Mother," he had said more than once before leaving home. "I'll write stories myself someday." What he meant was, "Write and get them published." Now at last, when he had been working on the paper for nearly six months, his success with the anonymous paragraphs emboldened him. He copied what he thought was one of his best essays on sheets of paper, intending to hand it to Mr. Turner for his approval at their next meeting.

But when the editor came to the shop the very next day, Joel could not screw up his courage to the point of showing the piece to him. He went to the house a day or two after that with the manuscript in his pocket, sat there tongue-tied, and came away without ever having mentioned it. Finally he signed his favorite pseudonym, "Marlowe," to it, set it up in type, and handed the proof and the manuscript to Mr. Turner with fingers that shook a little.

Editors in those days almost never wrote letters to would-be contributors. They simply answered them through the columns of the paper or magazine: "W.B.K.'s poem shows traces of talent, but needs more polishing before we can use it"; "Arabella C.—your manuscript is too absurd for words to describe"—things like that.

Mr. Turner pursued the same plan. Within an hour he came out to the shop, handed Joel the proofs and manuscript, and went away without a word. Joel found that his own article had been approved, but there was a new piece of copy for him to set up. It read:

Marlowe

The article over the signature of Marlowe is published, not because it is entirely up to the standard of *The Countryman,* but because, being the production of a young man not high in his teens, it evinces promise of what he may do if he will. If he will be laborious and careful in the composition and elaboration of his articles, and do his best every time, I will continue to publish for him. But should he become careless in his composition, I will close the columns of this journal against him.—In after life he will thank me for being very rigid with his productions.

Joel read the item through rather dizzily, then put it in the next week's paper. In after years he laughed over the absurdity of all this; he pretending to Mr. Turner that "Marlowe" was an anonymous, unknown person, and Mr.

Turner taking the cue and pretending that he did not know that "Marlowe" was working in his own shop and eating at his table.

But Joe took the stern warnings of Mr. Turner very seriously, and labored hard to improve his writing. The odd thing is that the first item in the paper to which he signed his own name was a recipe for making black ink. This happened just a few weeks after the Marlowe episode. The item was written as if from a correspondent. It addressed the editor as "Mr. Countryman" and said that the ink recipe "might be valuable to your readers owing to the scarcity of the fluid," and the signature was "J. C. Harris."

What a marvelous thing it was to see his own name in print! It made him happy, yet made him shiver with the responsibility of it. But it gave him a little more courage. Within a few days he wrote out another essay, this one entitled "Grumblers," and pretending to be taken from an ancient Arabic book entitled *Tellmenow Isitsoornot*. He signed his name to it "J. C. Harris," sought Mr. Turner in the library, and blushing from top to toe, he brought it forth with a trembling hand.

"M-M-Mr. T-Turner," he quavered, "h-h-here's a p-piece I've written—a—I—I thought it m-might be g-good enough—m-maybe you'd read it—a—I mean for the p-paper. . . ."

Mr. Turner, true gentleman that he was, did not even smile. "Thank you, Joel," he said gravely, accepting the paper. "I'll read it as soon as possible." No sooner had he left the house than Joel became convinced that the essay was probably the most terrible thing ever written, and that he was the most stupid and presumptuous fellow living, to think that he could get such stuff into print. Mr. Turner would laugh at it, he would come back and hurl it at the idiotic author's head.

But not so! At his very next call at the shop, Mr. Turner said, as soon as he entered, "That's a very good piece, Joel. I've decided to use it. There are two or three slight changes I would suggest, but—on the whole, a very good essay."

Joel stood transfixed, red as a beet, composing stick in hand, a capital letter A held shaking in air with the other, paralyzed with delight. It seemed to him that he could never in his life be any happier than he was at that moment. "J. C. Harris" had come before the world as an author.

CHAPTER EIGHT

Woodland Melodrama

OUT-of-door life was glorious, too. Joel made the acquaintance of a boy from a neighboring plantation, a year older than himself, who was just the type to be a boon companion for a nature lover. This was James Knox Polk Gaither, named in honor of a recent President of the United States.

"I got an uncle named James, too," he told Joel, "and to keep from gittin' us mixed up, they call me Jim-Poke."

The Gaithers, though prosperous plantation owners, were not cultured, as were the Turners, and Jim-Poke, though he was nearly fifteen when Joel first came to know him, could read only the simplest things in books for little children. Words of two syllables or more were apt to be too much for him. There were no schools out in the country then, and a child must either be taught at home or sent to town for schooling, else he had no education at all.

Jim-Poke could write his name—when he did, Joel said, the letters "looked as if they were wrestling with each other"—and that was about all he could do in the way of penmanship. His favorite way of writing his autograph was with a pointed stick in sand or dust, and he was very proud of this achievement. Whenever he and Joel in their forays came to a place where recent rain had washed sand into a smooth plane, Jim-Poke could never resist that inviting surface. He would get a stick and laboriously scrawl "James K. Polk Gaither" on it.

But though Jim-Poke lacked book learning, he had a keen mind and much learning of another sort; he was almost an encyclopedia on nature. He was a friendly soul, and ever afterward, Joel counted his acquaintance with this unlettered country boy as one of the most valuable of his early life.

Jim-Poke knew every road, path, and dim woodland trail in the whole neighborhood. He could find his way through the great and seemingly trackless swamps which bordered the Oconee River, not far away. Joel declared that there was not a bird or a tree in the woods with whose name and nature he was not acquainted. He knew where the finest wild strawberries grew, the best chincapins and chestnuts and persimmons. Sometimes, when they were on a ramble or a hunt, he would say, "Le's go down this branch. They's some fine bullaces grows down here." He meant muscadines, the luscious Southern fox grapes, first cousins to the scuppernongs.

"These ripens the earliest of any I know of," he would remark, "and if we don't git some of 'em, the 'possums will have 'em all."

On the ground under the tall forest trees over which the vines clambered and spread their small, delicate foliage, the boys would find some of the tough-skinned grapes lying singly, like nuts, and they would throw clubs up into the trees and bring others thudding down.

The birds could not hide their nests from Jim-Poke, nor

could the wild animals escape him—for he was an ardent hunter. He had a tame buzzard which he had taken from a nest when it was young and brought up as such a pet that if he would permit it, the ugly bird would sometimes follow him on a ramble, flying from tree to tree. He set traps for flying squirrels, and tamed them very quickly after he had made them captive. The fearless way in which he pounced upon and handled snakes astounded Joel until he discovered that Jim-Poke played with only the harmless ones.

"No, sir! Nothin' but blacksnakes and chicken snakes and such," said he. "Whenever I pick up somep'n pizen, like a moccasin or a spreadin' adder, I do it quick and hard. I'll show you next time I can ketch one."

Truly, his method with these reptiles was as startling as that with the others. He and Joel were walking through grass and weeds a few days later when Jim-Poke suddenly leaped forward and downward, made a grab at the earth and came up with the tail of a high-land moccasin in his hand. With a quick and powerful reverse movement of his arm, he snapped the reptile—zip!—as one cracks a whip, jerking its head almost completely away from its body. Joel saw him do this a number of times afterwards with venomous snakes.

"Always ketch 'em by the tail," he grinned at Joel, "but be sure you don't miss your grab."

"I don't think I'll try it," said Joel.

"Now, I'll hang this feller on this limb," said Jim-Poke, draping the moccasin's body over the bough of a sapling, "and hit'll bring rain. We need rain."

A few small superstitions like this were the only flaws in his nature knowledge. He firmly believed that hanging a dead snake on a fence or bough would cause rain to fall within twenty-four hours. Sometimes this didn't come to pass, and Joel would remind him of it. But Jim-Poke always had an explanation.

"That snake musta wriggled off that limb," he would say. "You know, a snake never dies till sundown, I don't keer what you do to it. You kin kill it at sunup in the mornin', mash it to a jelly or cut it in two, and it won't die till sundown nohow. That moccasin musta wriggled off'n that limb onto the ground, and of course that stops the rain from comin'."

Once when they were walking in the woods, Jim-Poke's keen eyes spied two large hawks circling above the trees ahead of them.

"Gimme your hankcher," he said in a low tone to Joel, "and git under that red haw bush. We'll have some fun with them hawks."

He himself crouched under another shrub, and with Joel's handkerchief doubled and held just in front of his mouth, he began to make a queer sound—a series of cries something like "Hoo! hoo! hoo-hoo!"

"Some kind of owl?" asked Joel in a whisper.

"Yeh—swamp owl," replied Jim-Poke. "Never hear one?"

"No."

"Watch the other birds hide theirselves." And truly, the cry had caused great consternation in woodland. There were quick flashings of wings here and there in the shades, and then all the smaller birds had vanished and their voices were hushed. But the two hawks, screaming with indignation, came flying toward the sound with their feathers

Jim-Poke suddenly leaped forward and downward, and made a grab at the earth.

ruffled, and were followed by a third one, all primed for battle.

Jim-Poke had given the call again and again. As the hawks swooped around the trees above the boys' heads, the caw of a crow was heard.

"Now you'll see some fun," muttered Jim-Poke. "Keep right still."

The crow, flying high, might have gone on its way had it not heard the hated owl cry. It alighted on the very tip of a tall pine, and then caught sight of the three hawks. Instantly, it sounded the "assembly" call. Joel could not detect any difference between these caws and the others, but to crow ears, they meant an emergency. Where they all came from was a mystery, but in a few seconds the air was a-whir with wings and the pine was dotted thickly with sleek, black bodies, while others dropped down into scrub oaks near by.

They couldn't discover the owl, but the hawks would do just as well for opponents, so it was "Up Crows, and at them!" Truly a battle royal—such cawing, screaming, squawking, and fluttering Joel had never heard or seen before. The hawks, badly outnumbered, finally fled the scene of action, after losing many feathers. But as they went—

"Look at that bee martin!" cried Jim-Poke.

He meant a kingbird or tyrant flycatcher, a little, scrappy fellow no bigger than a robin, but the Jack-the-Giant-Killer of the bird world. It darted down like a fighting plane from the skies, alighted on the back of one of the hawks, dug its claws into the flesh, and rode away on the big bird, tearing out beakfuls of feathers as it went.

The woodland melodrama was over. It had been so novel

and thrilling that Joel felt as if he had had a front seat at a real play.

"You cain't beat the crows," said Jim-Poke. "Smartest birds in the world; smarter'n some people I know. They're the only birds that'll gang together at a minute's notice when one of 'em hollers, and light into some other birds or whatever it is they wanta lick. They know what a gun is jest as well as you do. When they see a man with a gun, they'll git away from there a-callyhootin'."

Jim-Poke had two hounds, black and tan in color, named Jolly and Loud, which were almost as interesting to Joel as was their master. When Jim-Poke brought them over for Joel's first night hunt, Harbert went along, and even Mr. Wilson, but the latter fell over so many stumps and got into so many difficulties that he proved to be a nuisance, and never went again.

"Now, these are funny dogs," said Jim-Poke before they started. "If you start out with a light, they'll hunt 'possums all night long. If you go into the woods and fetch a whoop or two before you strike a light, they won't notice no 'possum, but you better believe they'll make ol' Zip Coon lift hisself off'n the ground. So whichever you want, you'll have to start out right."

Joel suggested 'coon, and with a whoop from Jim-Poke, they started into the woods in darkness, Mr. Wilson falling down now and then, and becoming impatient with the idea. Jim-Poke went on to explain the temperamental whims of the dogs.

"If Loud strikes a trail first," said he, "Jolly will pout—I call it poutin'. He'll run along with Loud, but he won't open his mouth until the scent gits hot enough to make him forget hisself."

The dogs had long since vanished from sight and hearing, and the hunters waited in silence only a few minutes before a far-off, mellow bay gave the news that Loud had found a trail. Sure enough, Jolly said nothing for a few minutes, until the trail became hotter.

"Now, le's light up," said Jim-Poke. They set fire to the pitch-pine torches and started on, but Jim-Poke called a halt again, that he might listen carefully.

"That 'coon has been caught out from home," he said after a pause. "The dogs are between him and his holler tree. He's makin' for that dreen in Pap's ten-acre field. There's a pond there, and old Zip has gone there after a bait of frogs. Jest wait till they turn his head this way."

Mr. Wilson ridiculed the notion that Jim-Poke could know all this just by listening to the distant voices of the dogs, but the young hunter went even further and said that the 'coon was about three-quarters of an hour ahead of the dogs—maybe a little more or less. He knew this by the fact that the dogs were not giving tongue as vigorously as they would when the trail became hotter.

"How do I know that 'coon is goin' away from home?" he repeated. "Shucks! My sev'm senses tell me that." He believed that the dogs would bring the animal back in their direction, and sure enough, they did—their voices proclaiming the fact that they were gaining on the quarry. They passed not far from where the hunters were waiting, and the latter promptly ran after them for another mile. Then Jim-Poke and Harbert both exclaimed:

"They've treed him!"—for now the dogs' voices took on a new sound. The men and boys reached the spot, and Harbert, who had brought his ax with him, felled the tree, which was not a large one. The raccoon daringly stole down the trunk and escaped as the tree struck the ground, and the dogs chased it for two miles more. Then their voices proclaimed to Jim-Poke's knowing ears that the 'coon had taken to water. They found him, a big fellow, treading water in a pool, with the dogs running around it, barking furiously.

"Fetch him out, boys!" ordered their master, and in they went—cautiously, for a big raccoon is a dangerous antagonist. They had their own artful plan of campaign. While Jolly swam around the animal, making feints at attack, Loud idled near by until the 'coon's attention was drawn from him; then he made a sudden dart and snap, and the battle was over.

Mr. Turner added to Joel's out-of-door enjoyment by giving him a colt to break and use as his own. Joel devoted much care to the training of this beautiful little animal, which he christened Butterfly.

There was a fox-hound pup, too, which came from the kennels of the celebrated Mr. Birdsong of south Georgia, who was a great admirer of *The Countryman* and its editor. Mr. Turner gave the dog to Joel to be trained. Mr. Birdsong wrote that the pup had been born under a gourd vine, so they called him Jonah.

"Mr. Birdsong breeds the only dogs around here that can catch the red fox," Mr. Turner told Joel. "Perhaps you didn't know that the red fox is not a native of this country. The gray fox is our American species, but dogs can catch it too easily. So in 1730 some gentlemen in Maryland decided to import some red foxes from England to give their dogs better sport. They did so and turned them loose, and now red foxes are scattered over most of the country east of the Mississippi River. Mr. Birdsong's dogs have become famous as hunters of this fox." (The Birdsong breed is famous to this day.)

Joel had great fun out of training Jonah. Almost every day he would drag a foxskin through wood and field for the pup to trail, or send a little Negro boy to do it while he followed with the dog. Before he was two years old, Jonah had tracked and caught a red fox unaided, and a little later he was the star of a neighborhood fox hunt.

Joel soon learned from Mr. Turner how he could make some pocket money.

"Mr. Wall needs rabbit fur for making hats," explained his employer. "He runs our little hat factory, though I'm backing him. You may take my rabbit dogs in your spare time and catch them, and you can make some traps and catch more. Wall will pay you fifty cents a dozen for the skins. There are so many rabbits around here that they are a great nuisance. They eat our green vegetables in the garden, and they gnaw the bark off young fruit trees and kill them. I'd be glad to have them thinned out."

So Joel took the little harriers and had many a chase, bringing in quantities of skins. Sometimes Jim-Poke accompanied him, and then it was more fun. He had to take his pay in paper money, of course, for there was no silver in circulation in the Confederate States, and nobody had seen any gold since the war began.

There were advertisements of the hat factory—always in Mr. Wall's name—in *The Countryman* every week:

HAT SHOP. Those who desire hats made, must have their orders entered upon my book, and they will be filled in their turn, as millers grind. Provisions and material are all the time going up, so that I cannot tell you what I will charge you. When the time comes to fill your bill, I will tell you my charge, and you can have your hat made, or withdraw your order. Positively no order will be attended to out of its turn. I can't even buy a band for your hat except for cash. If you haven't got the money to pay me, bring meat, corn, or other provisions, and they will answer in the place of money. . . . Good people of Putnam, encourage home industry, and let the old man live.

MILES S. WALL

Joel went over to the small frame building which housed the hat business and made the acquaintance of Mr. Wall—a quaint little old man who came from North Carolina, and was an ardent Baptist. But he was very superstitious; he believed in ghosts, witches, and werewolves, and saw signs in everything. If his nose itched, that meant that somebody was talking about him. When he had rheumatism in his left leg, he tied a rattlesnake skin around it, and believed that this eased the pain considerably. If a dog howled at night or a screech owl cried on the roof, he expected some ill fortune, probably death, to strike near by, perhaps at himself. But with all his queer beliefs, he was very orthodox in his religion.

"Whenever you hear anybody," he admonished Joel, "a-axin' anything 'bout how I'm gittin' on, an' how my fam'ly is, an' whether or no my health is well, you thess up an' tell 'em I'm a natch'al Babtist. You thess up an' tell 'em that, an' I'll be mighty much obleedge to you. Tell 'em I'm a borned Babtist.

"Most folks," he told Joel, "brings the wool or the skins in here—rabbit, 'coon, or beaver—and I make 'em into hats. But you cain't hardly git 'em to bring wool enough.

Mr. Turner says he's goin' to put a 'tisement in the paper, tellin' 'em to bring more wool than they think's enough. He's a-goin' to say to 'em, 'Your cheap scales is no 'count. They pull down about a pound before they begin to weigh anything. If you bring too much wool, you kin tote some of it back.' That's Mr. Turner! He don't mind tellin' 'em right to their faces."

"Do you get any beaver skins nowadays?" asked Joel.

"Hardly ever. I dunno whether they's any beavers left in Georgy now or not. We got three beaver hats left, an' it's goin' to be hard to sell 'em, they're so dear. 'Course, we only make the beaver into dress hats; plug hats, ye know. Up No'th, they make these here silk hats nowadays, but folks down in this neck o' the woods don't wear 'em; 'specially since this war come on, an' they cain't get 'em.

"Thess about the finest hat I ever made," said Mr. Wall, looking upward with dreamy eyes. "I made it fur Mr. John D. Tharp, Esquire, of Macon. Don't happen to know him, do ye? It was made outa beaver that was took right below Macon, an' it was a joe-darter, ef I do say it myself. But"—he paused and thumped angrily at a batch of wool on his table—"It was too big fur him. Consound him, he didn't medjure his head right! An' I cain't make hats to fit unless I git the right medjurements, kin I? He said he wouldn't 'a' took a hundred dollars fur that hat ef hit'd been the right size. As 'twas, he had to sell it."

Mr. Wall had other lines of business, too. He made shoe blacking—"Beauregard Blacking," he called it, in honor of a popular Southern general, and advertised it in *The Countryman* at twenty-five cents a pint. "It is liquid," his ads said, "and until I get my glass factory in operation, you must bring your bottles, and I will fill them."

Once in a while he sold a pint of the blacking.

"Spinnin' wheels, too," he told Joel. "Don't know of a lady wants a good spinnin' wheel, do ye? I got a couple nice new ones I'll sell fur five dollars each. A bargain!"

The method of making hats at this little factory was the same as it had been in England a hundred years and more before. One of Mr. Wall's three or four Negro helpers stretched a rabbit skin on a bench, fastened it, and scraped it with a knife.

"What you see on a rabbit when you looks at him," explained this man, "is de outer ha'r; long ha'r, an' it's too coarse for us to use in hat-makin'. We scrapes dat off, an' den we comes to de fine, soft fur nex' de skin. Jes' feel it— finer dan any ha'r you ever seed. Now, we takes dat off."

He slid a razor-sharp steel knife along the skin, shearing off the fluffy, delicate fur. When starting to make a hat, Mr. Wall would take sheep's wool or the fur from a great many skins and weigh it until he knew he had just the right number of ounces. Then he would heap it on the table and stir and fluff it until there seemed to be two or three times as much of it as at first. Next he began spreading and patting it into a big sheet.

"A little thicker nigh the edge than in the middle, ye see," he pointed out to Joel. "That's for the brim. It must be heavier an' stiffer than the crown. Mo' wear an' tear on it.

"Now, we call it a bat," he said when he had finished the spreading, "thess the same as you call a sheet of raw cotton a bat."

He laid a damp cloth over the sheet of fur and patted it gently all over, then laid a large piece of leather on the cloth and patted again. Finally he removed the leather, took hold of the middle of the cloth with his thumb and finger and lifted it quickly—and the whole sheet of fur came with it!

"Now we put it into the heatin' box," said Mr. Wall. "That makes the fur shrink."

There was a long process of heating in the box, of patting and kneading and occasional sprinkling with water. At last, the bat had been turned into a big, clumsy, flappy sort of conical affair. It didn't look as if it could ever be made into anything wearable.

"Now we call it a bonnet," said Mr. Wall.

Joel laughed. "It doesn't look like any bonnet I ever saw a lady wear," he said. "Looks more like the hat a clown wore in a circus that came to Eatonton a couple of years ago, only the clown's hat was a better shape."

"I seed that circus show," said Mr. Wall contemptuously. "Went all the way to town to see it, an' I wisht I'd 'a' saved my time an' money. Hit was the triflin'est thing I ever laid my two eyes on. Only one clown, an' him not very funny, an' about half a dozen hosses, an' no wild animals, an' the pe'fawmers all second rate. I wisht you could see the circus shows I've went to a coupla times in Raleigh. Had to go forty miles to see 'em, but hit was worth it. Why, a circus show wouldn't hardly dare to come to that town nowadays unlest it had a elephant."

The hat making went on. Mr. Wall passed the bonnets to the Negroes, who dipped them in boiling water, then pressed and kneaded them with tools something like small rolling pins. Every time the hot water touched the bonnets, they shrank still more under the rolling and kneading. Finally one of them was ready for Mr. Wall to place it on the block and shape it for the wearer's head. As the final

He laid a damp cloth over the sheet of fur, and patted it gently all over.

touches, Joel watched him sew the bands on it, inside and out.

"Now, thar's your hat," he said at last, holding it up proudly. "As han'some a job as you kin git in New York, if I do say it myself."

Mr. Wall was a good hat maker, but a poor business manager, so Mr. Turner presently took over the factory—everybody in the neighborhood knew that he practically owned it, anyhow—and put Mr. Wall on a salary as superintendent.

Now the advertising took on a different tone. As Mr. Wall said, Mr. Turner "didn't mind tellin' 'em!" "No hats made to order," was his new policy. "You can find them of all sorts and sizes, ready made, at the hat shop. I will not trade in Eatonton."

Another notice was still more blunt:

> Fur hats for sale, by retail. Call at the shop and get them, if you want them. I am not going to be hat peddler and haul hats backward and forwards to Eatonton any longer. You have already imposed too much upon my good nature. Quousque, tandem, abutere, Catilina, patientia nostra?— J. A. Turner.

And yet this man who was so gruff with his higher-class customers gave away more and more hats as the war went on, and the poor people in the country became poorer. Many a Confederate soldier went into battle wearing a Turnwold hat which was never paid for.

CHAPTER NINE

A Race of Song and Story Makers

WHEN Joel described to Harbert how the hawks and crows had bristled up and prepared for battle as soon as they heard what they thought was the cry of an owl, Harbert said, "Law, yes suh! Ain't you nebber hear de tale obut de owl an' de yuther birds?"

Joel hadn't, and Harbert told him why the owl is an outcast. Of course, it all happened long ago, before history began, when all the birds were "in cahoots," and had a community storehouse, where they put away all the foodstuffs that they could "ketch and fetch." But they discovered that some thief was stealing from their store, and decided that they must appoint a watchman to stand guard over it all day long.

After much powwow, Mr. Owl was chosen and took his post. But during the first day, Mr. Crow and Mr. Jaybird met and gossiped several miles away, and each admitted to the other that he doubted that Mr. Owl was fit for the job, because he was so sleepy-headed. They finally decided to fly back to headquarters and see how he was getting on, and there they found him so sound asleep that " 'twas all dey could do to wake him up."

The two reported the matter to the other birds, some of whom didn't more than half believe their story. But after much debate, it was decided to give Mr. Owl another chance. They gave him not only one but two more trials, and each time someone came back and found him fast asleep and some of the provisions stolen.

"Dat settle de hash for Mr. Owl," continued Harbert. "De birds set a day an' fotch Mr. Owl up for trial, an' dey laid down de law dat f'm dat time on, Mr. Owl shan't go wid de yuther birds, an' dat ev'y time dey kotch him out, de word was to be give, an' dey was all to fall foul on him an' frail him out. Den dey say dat when he sleep, he got to sleep wid bofe eyes wide open, an' dey lay it down dat he got to keep watch all night long, an' whensomever he hear any fuss, he got to holler out:

" 'Who—who—who pesterin' we all?'

"Dat's de way de law stan's," Harbert concluded, "an' dat's de way it gwine to stan'."

When Harbert repeated the words which the culprit was doomed forever to say, he gave so good an imitation of the hoot owl's cry in speaking them that Joel was greatly entertained.

The old Negro had much to tell his young friend of other things, too—of "patter-rollers" and runaway slaves, and adventures in the great canebrakes along the Oconee; things, some of which Joel afterward worked into his story, "Daddy Jake, the Runaway." The patroller—"patter-roller" as the Negroes called him—was a sort of neighborhood policeman who was most active at night. His job was to catch Negroes away from home without permission, those who went visiting or went to town and overstayed their leave, those who got drunk or stole from the neighbors or committed other misdemeanors. Joel observed that the patroller was seldom seen around the Turner plantation, where the Negroes were well behaved and gave very little trouble.

Harbert had a powerful yet musical voice, and when he sang or shouted on a still day with little moisture in the air, he could sometimes be heard for two miles. The calling of hogs on farms has always followed rather closely a certain set of sounds, but Harbert—or some earlier humble or gifted plantation minstrel—had taken these sounds and woven them into a song:

> Oh, rise up, my ladies, listen unto me,
> Gwoop! Gwoop! Gee-woop! Goo-whee!
> I'm a-gwine dis night fer ter knock along o' you
> Gwoop! Gwoop! Gee-woop! Goo-whoo!
> Pig-goo! Pig-gee! Gee-o-whee!

> Oh, de stars look bright, des like dey gwine to fall,
> En 'way tow'ds sundown you hear de killdee call;
> Stee-wee! Killdee! Pig-goo! Pig-gee!
> Pig! Pig! Pig-goo! Pig! Pig! Pig-gee.

> De blue barrow squeal kaze he can't squeeze froo,
> En he hump up his back, des like niggers do—
> Oh, humpty-umpty blue! Pig-gee! Pig-goo!
> Pig! Pig! Pig-gee! Pig! Pig! Pig-goo!

> Oh, rise up my ladies! Listen unto me!
> Gwoop! Gwoopee! Gee-woop! Goo-whee!
> I'm a-gwine dis night a-gallantin' out wid you!
> Gwoop! Gwoopee! Gee-whoop! Goo-hoo!
> Pig-goo! Pig-gee! Gee-o-whee!

Ole sow got sense, des as sho's you bo'n,
'Kaze she tak'n hunch de basket fer to shatter out co'n—
Ma'am, you makes too free! Pig-goo! Pig-gee!
Pig! Pig! Pig-goo! Pig! Pig! Pig-gee!

W'en de pig git fat he better stay close,
'Kaze fat pig nice fer ter hide out an' roas'—
En he taste mighty good in de barbecue!
Oh, roas' pig, shoo! 'N-Yum! dat barbecue!
Pig! Pig! Pig-gee! Pig! Pig! Pig-goo!

Oh, rise my ladies! Listen unto me:
Gwoop! Gwoopee! Gee-woop! Goo-whee!
I'm a-gwine dis night fer ter knock aroun' wid you!
Gwoop! Gwoopee! Gee-whoop! Goo-whoo!
Pig-goo! Pig-gee! Gee-o-whee!

Certain lines of this song, as may be guessed, were sung, while the "Gwoop! Goo-whee!" and the "Pig! Pig! Pig-goo! Pig-gee!" were whooped in the old-time calling style, so that the hogs a mile or so away in wood and field could hear it, and come, grunting and squealing, for their supper.

"Pig-goo! Pig-gee!" was not the only song whose words Joel preserved during those war years. At Turnwold and on other plantations which he visited, he heard plowhands' songs, joyous melodies of Christmas and of cornhusking time in autumn, serenades, play songs, and what we now call "spirituals," and he set the words of many of these down on paper, just because of the deep interest they had for him. He had not the faintest idea that some day he would publish them, and they would attract wide attention as quaint and beautiful expressions of a highly rhythmic, imaginative, and poetical race. It did not occur to him that in listening to these enslaved but joyous minstrels, he was laying the cornerstone of his career.

We have all seen pictures of Pan, the rural god of ancient Greek mythology, playing upon his Pandean pipes or teaching Apollo to do so. This instrument was just a row of reeds, usually about a dozen, of different lengths, fastened alongside one another, and the musician blew upon the tops of them to produce the music. As each pipe sounded only one note, the performer had to whisk the thing to and fro pretty rapidly in almost any sort of tune, and if he was playing a lively air, he was apt to jerk his head back and forth, too, in a way that was comical to onlookers.

How this ancient instrument descended to the Negro slaves of early American history is something that we cannot account for now. In Georgia it was called "the quills." The Negroes in Putnam County got the reeds from the Oconee canebrakes, cleaned the pith out of them, carefully cut them into lengths so that they were in tune, and lashed the little pipes together with cobbler's twine waxed with cobbler's wax so that it would not slip. Fontaine—usually called "Fountain"—a Negro on the Turner plantation, was an expert performer on the quills, and Joel found much pleasure in listening to him.

In fact, Joel and the Turner children, with whom he had become well acquainted, spent many of their evenings, both winter and summer in the "quarters," as the Negro cabins back of the big house came to be called, for there was always entertainment for them there—music on the Pandean pipes, singing, dancing, and, best of all to Joel, the stories of old Uncle George. Harbert and Uncle George were the chief storytellers of the plantation, and many an evening Joel spent by their fireside, while yams baked in the hot ashes, a corn pone browned, either in a "reflector" or on a shovel before the flames, and the old Negro, in the mellow, flowing dialect of his race, told the vivid myths of the wild things of wood and field, or softly sang one of the songs which Joel afterward made known to the world. Uncle George had an even greater fund of the animal yarns than Uncle Bob Capers, Joel's pal in Eatonton. Most of the Negroes cooked over an open fire, but Uncle George, who was a widower and lived alone, had an unusual feature at his cabin—a curious Dutch oven, in which he baked ginger cakes which were famous for miles around.

Every Saturday he baked a quantity of these cakes and sold them—in autumn, along with a drink made from wild persimmons and called persimmon beer—to the children of the neighboring plantations, who would come a long way to taste Uncle George's dainties and hear his quaint sayings.

The Turner children would drop in at his cabin in the evening while he was cooking his supper in that oven, and by the flickering firelight they would chat with him, listen to his stories and hoodwink him out of some of his sweets. He had ginger cakes all through the week, too, and though this was supposed to be an article of commerce with him, the children often succeeded in wheedling them away from him, together with juicy, baked yams, and goodness knows what not. Little Joe Syd Turner, slightly younger than Joel, but his favorite chum among the Turner children, was especially clever at this. Uncle George frequently grumbled that he was destined to "die in de po'-house," but he couldn't resist Joe Syd's blandishments.

On those evenings, while the lightwood knots blazed in the fireplace or under the oven, the children sat and heard those legends, whose first teller no one knows, but which followed a similar pattern among all the Negroes of the South. Br'er Rabbit, one of the smallest and weakest, certainly the most defenseless of animals, was by a sort of poetic justice, nearly always the hero. A confirmed practical joker, he was continually in hot water, and usually in peril of his life, but always managed to escape through his own shrewdness.

Br'er Fox and Br'er Wolf were the villains, and inevitably got their just deserts at the end of a story. They were killed time and again in the course of Uncle George's evenings, and he had to do a lot of explaining to account for these numerous deaths, for the children always wanted to know *why* the rascal was alive again, after having been scalded to death last week. Sometimes the old man had to wriggle out of his dilemma by changing the subject, or pretending to be offended, or announcing that the session was over for the evening.

Then there was Br'er Bar (the common black bear of the eastern United States was his original), big, clumsy, crotchety, slow-witted but commanding respect because of his size, sometimes on good terms with Br'er Rabbit, at other times angry at him and trying to kill him; Br'er Tarrypin (the land tortoise), also small and helpless but crafty and full of tricks, which enabled him to escape from tight places and the wiles of his enemies; stodgy old Sis Goose and Sis Cow—you could put almost anything over on them —Br'er 'Coon, Br'er 'Possum, Br'er Turkey Buzzard, and several more.

There were many ways of starting Uncle George on a

story. One of the Turner boys came in one evening with a paper box containing a crawfish, which he had captured in a brook running down into the swamp.

"Dem crawfishes is cu'ious critters," said Uncle George, shaking his head at the little thing as it scuffled about in the box. "Folks call 'em fish, an' yit dey ain't fishes. Some of 'em lives in de swamps an' branches an' some of 'em digs holes in de groun', an' lets it rain a little puddle at de bottom o' de hole, an' lives in dat. De ones dat lives in dem holes must be thinkin' 'bout de time wher der great-grand-daddies started de Flood."

"What flood, Uncle George?" asked Joel.

"De big Flood, honey. De one away back yonder. Hit was long befo' yo' daddies an' mammies was bawn. In dem days, de animals an' de beasteses had lots mo' sense dan what dey got now; let alone dat, dey had sense same like folks. Well suh, dey sorter 'lectioneered 'roun' mongst deyselves, till at last, dey 'greed for to have a 'sembly, to sorter straighten out matters an' hear de complaints.

"An' when de day come, dey was all on han'. De Lion, he was dere, 'ca'se he was de king, an' he had to be dere. De Rhinossyhoss, he was dere, an' de Elephant, he was dere, an' de Camels an' de Cows, an' plumb down to de Crawfishes, dey was dere. Dey was all dere. An' when de Lion shuck his mane an' tuck his seat in de big cheer, den de session begun fer to commence."

"What did they do, Uncle George?" asked Joe Syd, after an impressive pause.

"Well, suh, dey was so much of it dat I cain't skacely call to mind all dey did do, but dey spoke speeches, an' hollered, an' cussed, an' flung der languidge 'roun' des like when yo' daddy"—he looked at the Turner children—

"run fer de Legislatur' three, fo' year ago. Howsomever, dey 'ranged der 'fairs an' splained der business. Bimeby, w'iles dey was 'sputin' longer one anudder, de Elephant tromped on one o' de Crawfishes. Co'se, when dat creetur put his foot down, w'atsomever's under dere's boun' to be squshed, an' dey wasn't 'nough o' dat Crawfish left fer to tell dat he'd been dar.

"Dis make de udder Crawfishes mighty mad, an' dey sorter swa'med togedder an' drawed up a kinder peramble wid some wharfo'es in it, an' read it out in de 'sembly. But bless gracious! sech a racket was a-gwine on dat nobody ain't hear it, 'cep'n maybe de Mud Turkle an' de Spring Liza'd, an' deir infloonce was pow'ful lackin'.

"Bimeby, whiles de Nunicorn was 'sputin' wid de Lion, an' whiles de Hyener was laughin' to hisse'f, de Elephant squshed anudder one o' de Crawfishes, an' a little mo' an' he'd 'a' ruint de Mud Turkle. Den de Crawfishes, what dey was left on 'em, swa'med togedder an' drawed up anudder peramble wid some mo' wharfo'es; but dey might as well 'a' sung Ol' Dan Tucker to a harrycane. De udder creeturs was too busy wid der fussin' to pay any 'tention. So dar de Crawfishes was, an' dey didn't know what minute was gwine to be de nex'; an' dey kep' on gittin' madder an' madder an' skeerder an' skeerder, till bimeby dey gin de wink to de Mud Turkle an' de Spring Liza'd, an' den dey bored little holes in de groun' an' went down outer sight.

"Yes suh, dey bored into de groun' an' kep' on borin' ontil dey unloosed de fountains o' de earf, an' de waters squirt out, an' riz higher an' higher till de hills was kivered, an' de creeturs was all drownded; an' all 'ca'se dey let on 'mong deyselves dat dey was bigger dan de Crawfishes."

Uncle George drew a hot yam from the fireplace, blew the ashes from it and proceeded to remove the peeling.

"Where was the ark, Uncle George?" asked the little Turner girl.

"Which ark's dat?" asked Uncle George, with an affectation of surprise and curiosity.

"Noah's ark," was the reply.

"Don't you pester wid ol' man Noah, honey," said Uncle George, shying away from the subject, as usual when he was caught in a tight place. "I be bound he took keer o' dat ark. Dat's what he was dere for, an' dat's what he done. Leastways, dat's what dey tells me. But don't you bodder 'long o' dat ark, 'ceptn de preacher brings it up."

"But Uncle George," protested Joe Syd, "the Bible says the flood happened because it rained forty days and forty nights." Joe Syd hadn't yet learned, as Joel had, to take these old legends as they were, without question.

"As to dat," said Uncle George with stiff dignity, "dey mought 'a' been two delooges, an' den ag'in dey moughtn't. If dey was any ark in dis yer w'at de Crawfishes brung on, I ain't hear tell on it, an' when dey ain't no arks aroun', I ain't got no time for to make 'em an' put 'em in dere. Hit's gittin' bedtime for little chillen."

CHAPTER TEN

Young Oliver Goldsmith

JOEL had been working on *The Countryman* only a
few months when Mr. Turner wrote an editorial
which had a great influence upon his career. It began:

I do emphatically wish us to have a Southern literature.
And prominent in our books I wish the negro placed. The
literature of any country should be a true reflex in letters of
the manners, customs, institutions, and local scenery of that
country. Hence when our authors write I don't believe they
ought to run off to Greece, Rome, the Crusades, England, or
France for things for their pens. Let them write about things
at home and around them.

Joel pondered that editorial, and it influenced his future
thinking. He became a booster for Southern literature, and
he gave his attention to subjects near home, things about
which he knew instead of trying to write about Italian bandits and Western Indians. Years, later, he was to remember
what Mr. Turner said about the Negro, too.

But at the time, even if it had occurred to him that something literary might be made out of his experiences with

his colored friends, there would have been no market for what he might write. The South was too busy with the war, and the Negro was still too much of an everyday subject, and too closely connected with the causes of the war; people wanted to think about something else.

Finally, dialect stories, such as he wrote in his later years, were not considered quite dignified then, and Joel in his teens was very firmly determined not to get off his literary dignity. His aspirations were lofty. The sparkling humor which flowed so freely from his pen when he was working on other newspapers a few years later was not in evidence now. Instead, most of the things he brought out from his old notebook or wrote anew were deadly serious, and some even somber.

One of the articles—which he had written some time before—was entitled, "Sabbath in the Country," and began:

> People who live in the crowded cities, as a general thing, have no idea of the beautiful stillness of a Sabbath evening in the country, far away from the bustle and turmoil attendant on city life. In the city, one cannot read or worship God as he would choose. He must needs be interrupted; while in the country, it is the reverse. . . .

Fancy that, from a youth who had never in his life seen a town larger than Eatonton! Incidentally, the "crowded cities" in 1863, with their tree-shaded streets, with no automobiles or apartment houses, no elevated or subway lines, no telephones or radio or motion pictures, no airplanes buzzing overhead, would seem almost rural to us today.

The strangest subject of all for a boy of fourteen to choose was "Death." This essay appeared in *The Countryman*

early in 1863, when he had not been working on the paper
a year. It began:

> What is death, that we so much fear it? Is it the end of
> man? Is it an end to all his troubles? Is it a long, eternal
> sleep—and is this why we all dread it?—These are the ques-
> tions that come looming up before the mind of every one. . . .

From such work as this, one might get an impression of
the writer as a solemn, owlish sort of person who saw no
fun in anything. On the contrary, Joel, when away from
his writing, was one of the merriest lads that ever lived,
and he continued so throughout life. His choosing of those
sober subjects was the result of his belief that he was destined to become as essayist—one like Oliver Goldsmith, he
hoped. Several years more were to pass before he realized
that he was a born humorist.

But that impish humor which expressed itself in his
everyday actions now began to beg for expression through
his writing, too. Still he held it back, but he wrote down
in the old composition book a little jingle—it never saw
print—which shows that he had begun to smile at sentimentality:

> Of all the flowers that grow in dirt,
>   I own I hate the rose,
> For "roses have their thorns" and I
>   Stuck one into my nose.
>
> I know also the lily is
>   In virgin dress bedight;
> But if that color suited me,
>   Why, geese are just as white!

The poet rants of verdant fields,
  And of the sky serene;
But I've seen Yankees just as blue,
  And boobies just as green.

He talks of love, that passion blent
  With heavenly pleasure sweet,
But as for me, I've always loved
  A dish of cold fried meat!

For the rest of his life, whenever Joel heard anyone beginning to gush or trying to get him to do so, he was apt to turn the thing to ridicule by a quip like that in the last line of his poem.

He now began to break out in a rash of puns, some of which Mr. Turner let him slip into the paper, as by "The Countryman's Devil." A typical one was this, which plays upon the political relations of two Georgia politicians:

Why must Governor Brown's reputation as commander-in-chief of our forces grow less?

Because for all his military reputation he is obliged to Wayne.

Some other papers began to joke about this, and Mr. Turner cracked back at one of them, *"The Confederate Union* is disposed to undervalue the services of *The Countryman's* devil. If it only knew what a smart devil *The Countryman* has, it would not do so. Just ask your 'Jim' about it, Brother Nisbet. He knows our devil."

This meant that young Jim Harrison, who had worked

for *The Countryman* for a while, had gone over to the other paper.

Joel loved to write on subjects relating to literature. Mr. Turner let him do a number of reviews and criticisms of the work of others then writing in the South. These, like his other productions at the time, were never written out with pen or pencil, but composed by him in type.

One of his favorite Southern writers was Captain Harry Lyndon Flash, who was born in Ohio, but who, after several years of study and travel in Europe, had settled in Georgia and become an ardent upholder of the Southern cause. He was editor of the *Macon Daily Confederate* during the war, and wrote poetry and essays also. Joel greatly admired his concise style, and called it "nervous condensation." In *The Countryman* of June 1864, he wrote an article on Flash's poem which opened in the manner of a reviewer or critic for one of the most dignified literary magazines:

> Dryden, I believe, has remarked upon the delicacy of visiting criticism upon living men. In view of this, I shall not attempt to criticise any of the productions of Mr. Flash, but merely give the readers facts in my knowledge which, I doubt not, every admirer of Southern genius will be glad to know, believing that if there was ever a time when the South should fully atone for her former coldness to her sons of song (and in fact, to all her authors), that time is now.

He went on to compare two or three of Flash's poems with those of Poe, and declared that in one poem, "He has told in twelve lines what some authors could not tell in twelve hundred."

A modern critic exclaimed in amazement, "It does not seem possible that this is the work of a fifteen-year-old boy." It seems still more amazing when we think of that boy an hour or so after writing it, whooping through the broom-sedge fields with the illiterate Jim-Poke Gaither on a rabbit hunt, or sitting with the Turner children in Uncle George's cabin, munching gingerbread and listening to tales of Br'er Rabbit and Br'er Fox and Br'er 'Possum. The quotation from Dryden—who is too dry even for most adults to wade through today—proves how much reading of the classics in the Turner library the boy had been doing since coming to the plantation.

But Joel did not always please Mr. Turner with his efforts. On one occasion he wrote an article—taking for his text an essay of Captain Flash's—which he turned over to the editor. A few days later he found the manuscript back on his table, together with this scorching note from Mr. Turner:

For the first time since you sent in this article I have found time to examine it, and though it has merit, I regret that I have to reject it, because it is not up to the standard of the "Countryman." In the first place, you have made a bad selection in the article you have chosen for a subject. That article is contemptible and beneath criticism. It borders on idiocy. Captain Flash did his paper injustice in publishing it. In the next place, there is want of unity and condensation in your article. It is headed "Irishmen—Tom Moore," and then goes off on a great variety of subjects, and is too diffuse on everything it touches.

In writing hereafter, 1st select a good—a worthy subject.
2nd, stick to that subject.

3d, say what you have to say in as few words as possible.
Study the "nervous condensation" which you so much ad-
mire in Captain Flash.

All this is for your good.

August 21st, 1864.   J. A. TURNER

This note cast the young author into deep gloom for an
hour or so. But he knew that Mr. Turner, as he said, meant
the criticism kindly, and he knew that the blunt, out-
spoken editor was a pretty good judge of literary productions. So he presently took heart, and began trying to write
something more worthy. All his life, Joel was very humble
about the quality of his work. If an editor told him that a
piece was bad, he usually admitted that the editor probably
knew what he was talking about.

It was a great comfort to him shortly afterward when
Mr. Turner took up the cudgels in his behalf, and wrote
with a touch of the contempt which he was apt to display
when he was angry:

> The gentleman (we forget his name) who is writing some
> articles for the Raleigh *Mercury* on the literature of the
> South . . . uses pretty freely an article of our young cor-
> respondent, Joel C. Harris, and yet never gives that corre-
> spondent the credit which is his due.

Mr. William Turner, who was sent home from the army
in 1863 because of a wound, also took a deep interest in
the young scribe's literary development. He continued to

"oversee" the ancestral plantation in his easygoing way, but became associate editor of *The Countryman,* which had now grown to a sixteen-page paper, though the pages were somewhat smaller than at first.

"Here's something that may be of use to you, Joe," said he one day, handing the boy a book. It was Parker's *Aids to English Composition,* and· on the flyleaf was written "William W. Turner to J. C. Harris."

Despite its increased size, *The Countryman* had not room for all the ideas which came trooping through Joel's brain, and many things that he wanted to say were not suitable to that paper, so he began—very timidly at first—sending them elsewhere in the South. He could not have gotten them through to Northern editors, and they might not have been accepted if he had.

He was still boy enough to enjoy writing an occasional story about and for children, and he sent these, for the most part, to Sunday-school papers. "Charlie Howard; or Who is the Good Boy?" was a typical subject which appeared in the *Child's Index,* a Baptist Sunday-school paper published in Macon.

To adult papers and magazines he sent literary and political articles, stories, satire, and now and then a poem. He was very modest, as might be expected about these things. One letter will prove this:

EDS. COMMONWEALTH:—

SIRS: I send you an article for the "Commonwealth," which, if you see fit, publish, otherwise burn it up. On no account let my name be known. Hoping that you may soon receive a thousand reams of nice paper (which is the best wish that any paper can receive nowadays); I remain

Your friend,

J. C. HARRIS

P.S. I have an original composition for the "Commonwealth" entitled "A Night Hunt." Must I send it?

J. C. H.

At times he jotted down in his old scrapbook a sort of summary of his literary work for some weeks past, and an item in it in 1863—when he was not yet fifteen—shows how busy he was at composition:

Don't recollect when I finished "Doodang." The "Southern Watchman" copied it under the head of "Select Miscellany"!!!—Finished "Laughing Corpse" June 14th, have not sent it off, yet. Finished "Gran'pap" the same day. Have not sent it off yet. Will send it to "Child's Index." Finished "A Night's Hunt" three weeks ago. Have not sent it off yet. No literary papers to send it to in the South, now that the "Fireside" had stopped. I am engaged on a "Burlesque," though that is not its name. It shall be in ridicule of the Yankees, and of the South, too, for not advancing literature; do what I can to help the cause along, people will not patronize *our* papers.

Remember that for not one of these pieces did the author receive a cent of pay. There were comparatively few publications at that time which paid for the material they used—certainly none in the South during the war. Most writers, both North and South, had to be content for their reward with seeing their work in print and being read by the public.

Joel wrote political satires and burlesques which did not find their way into type, and no doubt he was glad of it afterward. One of these was a scathing letter to President Lincoln in rustic dialect—apparently Joel's first attempt in that form. Another was a play which was never completed, but which was to hold up to public odium the Northern General Butler, who was military governor of New Orleans for a time during the war. There was also a poem in another vein, an "Ode to Jackson, the Martyr of the South."

After he had seen his own name in print in *The Countryman,* Joel's confidence increased rapidly. Emboldened by the fact that the editors to whom he was sending his manuscripts did not know how young and rustic he was, he even became a bit cocky and ventured to criticize some of the publications for which he wrote. From a letter written to the *Illustrated Mercury* when he was sixteen, it is evident that he took such a deep interest in the paper which published his productions that he felt almost as if he were part owner of it. He said:

I like the "Mercury" exceedingly well, with the exception of one thing, if I may be allowed to be candid—and that is the illustrations. After you get your paper to paying, I hope you will discard them altogether. I am anxious for the "Mercury" to succeed, as I believe it is the only publication in the State, with the exception of the "Countryman" which does not model itself on the vile publications of the North, as for instance, the "Field and Fireside." I am afraid, also, that our Southern writers are giving way to a wholesale imitation of Yankee authors, especially the younger portion of those afflicted with the *cacoethes scribendi.* . . . Hoping that you may succeed in your endeavors to establish an undefiled Southern literature, and that the "Mercury" may prove a blessing to the "Confederacy," I remain,

Your well-wisher,

JOEL C. HARRIS

"Cacoethes scribendi"—that is, the "itch for writing," indeed! Certainly, Joel was getting on—flinging Latin about as if he had been a Bachelor of Arts!

CHAPTER ELEVEN

War Times

FOR a long time the Civil War seemed far away from Middle Georgia. To be sure, every little while news came that someone from Putnam County had been dreadfully wounded or killed; perhaps a boy not much older than Joel and whom he had known at Eatonton. He wrote or rather composed in type obituary notes of some of these, casually throwing in some bitter remark about the Yankees in the course of them. He—who after he became a well-known writer was the most tolerant of men and did all he could in his writings to dispel the prejudice and ill feeling between the North and the South—was a fiery partisan in his teens, as boys usually are, and could see no justice whatsoever on the Northern side of the quarrel.

Mr. Turner's plantation was almost a little world in itself. It could produce its own food and clothing, but even it began to feel the pinch of war. Coffee became very scarce all through the country, and many people were drinking substitutes made of parched corn meal, sweet potatoes shredded and dried, parched rye, parched okra seeds, or chicory. More tea made from sage and sassafras roots was drunk than ever before. Joel's favorite beverage was water sweetened with sorghum molasses, and he found it very pleasant and refreshing. Salt, which was not produced in the South, also became very scarce and costly. One day the Negroes heard that over on the Gaither plantation they had dug up the earthen floor of the smokehouse—saturated with years of drippings from the salt meat hung to its rafters—and were boiling it to get the salt out of it.

"Well, I'll have to be more hard up than I am yet before I'll do that," said Mr. Turner. "We're nearly out of salt right now, and I don't know where we are going to get more, but I've about come to the conclusion that salt is an unnecessary luxury anyhow."

"I just don't see how you can cook without salt," sighed Mrs. Turner. "I would think it would be necessary to our health."

"Not at all," declared Mr. Turner. "Look at the savage tribes all over the earth. None of them use a particle of salt in their food. Most of them never heard of salt. It's just unnecessary flavoring, like pepper or vanilla, and if worst comes to worst, I can get along without it."

"But how are you going to cure meat?" persisted Mrs. Turner.

"We'll just have to smoke it more," he answered.

Joel understood most of the difficulties of the South very well. He read in other papers of the blockade of Southern ports by the Northern warships, which prevented merchant ships from taking the South's chief product, cotton, out to sell to England and also prevented ships from bringing in coffee and sugar and salt and kerosene and, what was highly important to Joel, paper for printing. Paper became enormously expensive, but stranger still, things which they grew and made at home—food and clothing and shoes—

became costly, too. The price of rabbit skins rose until Joel was being paid twenty cents apiece for them—all in paper, of course—and he thought he was getting rich. But the queer thing was, that the more plentiful the paper money became, the higher prices were for everything you had to buy in the stores. Mr. Bryant, who owned a plantation near Turnwold and whose Negroes made quantities of the common cloth called jeans, worn by Negroes and the poorer class of white men, put an advertisement in *The Countryman,* offering it for sale at twenty dollars a yard.

"I'm going to be compelled to raise the price of *The Countryman* again," said Mr. Turner to Joel one day.

The subscription rate had been a dollar a year at the beginning. A few months later it was raised to five dollars, and then to ten.

"I'm losing money on it now," added the publisher, "and I can't keep on. I think I'll just announce the new rate as 'Five dollars for four months.' That won't sound so bad as fifteen dollars a year. I'll lose some subscribers, but it can't be helped."

"Why is everything so expensive, Mr. Turner?" asked Joel.

"Because our money is cheap," replied his friend. "It's always that way, Joel." He held his two hands in front of him, imitating the balances of a primitive scale. "When one goes up, the other comes down. Now our money is cheap, which means that everything you buy at the store is high. When we have a panic, as we had in the United States six years ago, money becomes scarce and high, and then goods are cheap. I'll loan you a book written by an old Scotchman named Adam Smith which will tell you about it."

"But why is our money cheap now?" asked Joel.

"Because our bankers and businessmen, because nobody has any confidence in it. Look at this paper money." He held out a ten-dollar bill. "You see that it's just a promise to pay ten dollars to anyone who brings it to the Confederate treasury two years after the signing of a treaty of peace with the United States. At first, when we thought we could lick the Yankees overnight, the notes promised to pay six months after the signing of such a treaty. Now we see that it's going to be a much tougher job, and we know that our government treasury has very little gold and silver; that these notes are just based on hope. And the worst of it is that our government keeps right on printing this so-called money, which for that reason grows less and less valuable all the time. Our State of Georgia money is still less reliable. That's the trouble—when you start inflation you can't stop."

Joel was downcast. He was thinking of all that paper money he had stowed away in his trunk upstairs from the sale of rabbit skins and the savings from his own wages. Mr. Turner guessed what was passing through his mind.

"I'll raise your wages and price of rabbit skins again, Joel," said he, "though it's becoming harder all the time for me to make ends meet. But if our armies can win some victories, if we can break the blockade and sell some cotton to Europe, if we can raid the North and get some cash out of those big banks up there, why, maybe we'll make our money worth something."

It was only a short time after this that news began to come of the great battles around Chattanooga, at first joyously proclaimed as Southern victories. But after two months the Northern army was in possession of the city and the surrounding mountains. This was at the northwest corner of Georgia, the closest yet that the great and bloody struggle of armed men had come to Putnam County. But then the two armies settled down where they were for the winter, and again middle Georgia, with enough to eat, such as it was, in the barns, cellars, and smokehouses, took life rather easily. That the soldiers were not faring so well is proven by an appeal from the Quartermaster General of Georgia, which appeared in *The Countryman* and other papers in February 1864:

> Daughters of Georgia! I still need socks. I still have yarn to furnish. I earnestly desire to secure a pair of socks for every barefooted soldier from Georgia. You are my reliance. Past experience teaches me that I will not appeal to you in vain.

Spinning wheels turned, knitting needles clicked, and looms thumped on every plantation. There were no longer any new silk dresses for the ladies; their cloth was made at home. Young women made their hats of rye and wheat straw, and some very pretty bonnets from the lacy fiber which enclosed the seeds in the hollow of what was called the "bonnet" squash.

The Confederate government allowed the farmer to plant only a limited number of acres in cotton, so that most of the land could be given to the growing of foodstuffs. Next came a law by which the government could seize as much of the farmers' grain and meat and hay as it thought necessary for its armies, leaving him just as little as it thought he and his family could get along on. This brought some queer dishes into existence—persimmon bread, for example. In autumn, the pulp of ripe persimmons was liberally mixed with corn meal to make bread. Joel found that he soon tired of it; in fact, there came a time when his stomach absolutely turned against it. Potato pone—sweet potatoes, boiled, mashed, and kneaded, formed into little loaves and baked wasn't so bad.

At Turnwold, the vegetable dish at some times of the year was a mixture of collards, turnip greens, and the young shoots of the pokeberry plant. This was boiled for noon dinner, and the leftover part fried for supper. It was called *callalou* by old Jimsy, the cook, its inventor. He had been born in the West Indies. His real name was Zimzi, and he was very sensitive; he ran away when anybody scolded him, but always came back in a day or two.

Already the government had been drafting men for the Confederate army, and now a law was passed by which it might seize horses, cattle, anything necessary for the support of the army or government. Some cattle were taken from the farms in Putnam County, but for a time life seemed to Joel to move along about as smoothly as usual. Sure enough, many of the subscribers of *The Countryman* had ceased to take the paper, and work wasn't quite so hard on press days. But in May came the news that the Confederate army under General Johnston was being rapidly pushed back from Chattanooga toward Atlanta by the Yankees under General Sherman.

Again the price of *The Countryman* rose, this time to twenty dollars a year.

Bad news came to Joel in letters from his mother and others. One from Hut Adams, now twenty years old and in the Quartermaster Department at Macon, addressed Joel as "Syksey," and jested about his job:

I trust you will not attribute my backward-git to any demoralization on my part, but remember that I am in the Q.M.Dept., and it is the first law of that heroic tribe to keep as far removed from danger as possible, for we are too important an institution to lose. Kill the Quartermaster! Why, the thought is too horrid to contemplate. Who would wear the gold lace, drive fast horses, etc.? Bully for the life-insured, bomb-proof Department!

Farther on he became serious, and said:

You asked me about the boys of those good old days now gone. There have been sad changes. Eli Awtry and Jim Johnson were killed in the late fight at Spottsylvania Court-House. I don't know where Gordon Whiting can be; he was nearly dead from Consumption the last I heard of him. Old Siddon you can't kill. Always foremost in the fight, he has passed through a dozen battles unscathed.

Late in July the news was that Johnston's army was in Atlanta and almost encircled, that Johnston had been replaced by General Hood.

A cousin of Joel's wrote from the battlefield there during the occasional "hissing of the minie-balls passing over our trenches. . . . The enemy are within 300 yards of our works. Their Sharp Shooters frequently greet us with unpleasant messengers, they also send a great many shell, which are very annoying but inaffective."

About this time some Federal raiders made a dash through Putnam County. As Mr. Turner had been attacking the Northern government pretty strongly in *The Countryman,* he was a marked man, and might have been roughly handled if they had caught him. As he wrote humorously a week later:

"It seemed evident that we must become *non comeatibus in swampo* (whither we retired) or be made prisoner. The female portion of our family decided the former was better for us, and we acted upon the suggestion." Then Joe Wheeler's gray-coated cavalry came along and drove the enemy raiders away, "and we have emerged, to finish our notes in our sanctum."

Some Negroes from plantations near by followed the raiders back to Atlanta and became hangers-on of the Northern army, but none forsook Turnwold. Many plantation owners feared an uprising of their slaves. Some of them were talking to Mr. Turner about it every few days.

"Remember the Negroes have the whites outnumbered three to one in this county," they would say. "If they should start an insurrection, they could make mince-meat of us. It would be just like the Yankees to supply them with guns."

"I don't think they will rise," said Mr. Turner, laughing comfortably. "I'm sure mine won't. If a man treats his Negroes kindly, he has nothing to fear from them."

Still there was great nervousness in the neighborhood as the siege of Atlanta went on. But Joel continued to compose his little essays in type, not much perturbed. One day Mr. Turner came back from Eatonton, and said, "They're fighting at Jonesboro, sixteen or eighteen miles south of Atlanta. That's only about sixty miles from here."

"Getting too close for comfort," said Mr. Wilson.

They would step out of doors now and then to see if they could hear the sound of cannon. Mr. Turner, anxious for news, went to town or sent Harbert almost every other day. Early in September the word came that Atlanta had fallen into the hands of the enemy; then there was a period of quiet. Presently a neighbor came one day to report, "Hood's gone back toward Chattanooga with Sherman after him, but Sherman left a part of his army at Atlanta."

"Well, I guess we'll not be bothered with them for a while," said Mr. Turner.

"What's a wool hat worth now?" asked the neighbor, after they had talked of the war for a while.

"Forty dollars."

The man whistled. "I reckon one made of 'coon fur would be plumb out of sight."

"They'd be higher, of course," said Mr. Turner, glancing at a copy of his paper which he held in his hand. "I've just written an advertisement of my hat business in this week's *Countryman,*" he continued. "Here are the prices I quote. I'd have to charge you $80 for a rabbit hat, $110 for one of 'coon fur, and $160 for a beaver."

"Laws a-mercy!" exclaimed the man. "I guess I'll have to get along with this old wreck I'm wearin'—unless you'd take barter for a new hat."

"Be glad to have it," said Mr. Turner, consulting his paper again. "I'll give you a wool hat for two-thirds of a beaver skin and pay you the difference; or I'll swap a wool hat for two pounds of clean, washed wool, three bushels of corn, a bushel and a half of wheat, ten pounds of lard, twelve 'coon skins, fifteen muskrat skins, twenty mink skins, or thirty rabbit skins. A rabbit hat will be worth double as much, a 'coon hat a third more than a rabbit hat, and a beaver double the price of rabbit."

Fancy two pounds of wool or three bushels of corn being worth forty dollars! But, of course, on the other hand, that money wasn't worth much more than the paper it was printed on.

That advertisement of the hat factory appeared in *The Countryman* for September 27, 1864, in the same number with Joel's first published poem. He had first written it when he was eleven. Since then, he had rewritten it and changed words and phrases in it time and again. Finally he submitted it to Mr. Turner, and it was accepted. It had the somber turn which appeared in most of Joel's writing during these years:

Nelly White

The autumn moon rose calm and clear,
   And nearly banished night,
While I with trembling footsteps went
   To part with Nelly White.

I thought to leave her but awhile,
   And, in the golden west,
To seek the fortune that should make
   My darling Nelly blest.

For I was of the humble poor,
   Who knew that love, though bold,
And strong, and firm, within itself,
   Was stronger bound in gold.

And when I knelt at Mammon's shrine,
   An angel ever spake
Approvingly—since what I did,
   I did for Nelly's sake.

Again I neared the sacred spot,
  Where she and I last met,
With merry laugh, does Nelly come
  To meet her lover yet?

            .   .   .

Again the moon rose in the sky,
  And gave a fitful light,
Which shone with dreary gleam upon
  The grave of Nelly White.

How strange that little poem looks now, by contrast
with the thunder of the war not so many miles away!
It proves that its author's mind was occupied with other
things than war.

The weeks went on pleasantly for Joel, for never in his
life was he a worrier, and now he was doing just what he
wanted to do—composing something every week for the
paper, hunting, trapping, rambling between times. As he
had enough to eat and wear, he did not realize how con-
ditions were beginning to pinch Mr. Turner. Crops had
been good. The Southern army had taken a great deal of
the grain and cured meat, but left some still in the cribs
and storehouses. There were hogs waiting to be killed
whenever the first cold snap came on, chickens and turkeys,
fruit and vegetables. To easygoing Joel, trouble seemed
far away.

CHAPTER TWELVE

Storm Clouds

BUT one day while Harbert was cleaning and oiling the old press in the printing office, he said to Joel, "De Yankee ahmy'll be comin' thoo heah befo' long."

"Oh, pshaw!" exclaimed Joel. "What would they be coming down this way for? There's nobody here for them to fight. Hood's army is on the other side of Sherman, away over in Alabama or Tennessee."

But Harbert was unmoved by his objections. "De word done come," was all he would say. "Hit's obleedged to be so, ca'se all de niggers done hear talk on it."

Joel knew that news traveled mysteriously, sometimes it seemed as if through the air, by way of the Negro quarters from plantation to plantation. Often it proved to be just idle gossip; even the more intelligent Negroes laughed at such talk and called it "nigger news." But in many cases it was correct. It was called over rail fences from one field to another by workmen, chattered by Negro women visiting from one plantation to another.

Just how the humble slaves learned of Sherman's intention to march toward the sea before the march began, before the whites knew it, has remained unexplained to this day. Even after the army started on that fateful march, some of the white people far down the state refused to believe that it was coming.

"I don't 'spect dey goin' ter bodder folks what don't bodder dem, is dey?" asked Harbert, still working on the press.

"I don't know," said Joel carelessly. "I guess not." He mentioned Harbert's remark to Mr. Turner when he saw him later that day, and he could see that his employer was very much impressed. The news spread rapidly in the vicinity, and all sorts of wild rumors followed. A few days later, Harbert had a confirmation of his story.

"Dey's on de way," he said, "comin' f'm Atlanta on forty diffe'nt roads—millions an' millions of 'em, an' headin' right for Putnam County."

Joel could not understand why. "Are they running away from our men?" he asked Mr. Turner.

"No," was the reply. "Our army has gone to Tennessee, and there are plenty of Yankees there to fight it." He pulled his beard thoughtfully. "Sherman may be heading toward the seacoast," he said slowly. "Aiming to cut our country in two. If he comes, we're going to lose a lot of our horses and cattle and provisions. But I'll have to have better information before I'll believe he's coming through here."

He went to his dwelling house, however, gathered up all the best of the family silverware, and put it into gunny sacks. Then he called Harbert out away from the house and said, "Harbert, this evening after dark I want you to bring Hector to the kitchen door. We're going to bury the silver in the woods." He believed that Hector was as faithful as Harbert and would help keep the secret. So that evening he and the two Negroes, Mr. Turner carrying the pick and shovel while the two others shouldered the heavy bags of tableware, went out in the forest and in the midst of a dense thicket buried the bags.

"Now you boys be sure you don't tell a soul where this is," said Mr. Turner. "Not even your families."

"No suh, we won't," they promised, and they were true to their word.

Negro messengers on horseback began galloping in now and then, bringing notes from neighboring plantation owners, telling of what they had heard. Then perhaps the messenger would ride on, carrying the same note to two or three other neighbors.

On Wednesday, the sixteenth of November—those dates were burned indelibly into Joel's brain for life—one of these men came spurring in through the wagon gate, his horse's hoofs throwing mud high in air. He rode to the "big house," as the Negroes called the Turner dwelling, and in a few minutes rode away again.

"What's the news, Colonel?" asked Mr. Wilson, when Mr. Turner came to the shop shortly afterward.

"Note from Mrs. Reid," said Mr. Turner. "She lives just over the line in Jasper County, west of here. Says report is the Yankees are coming, and she thinks of sending her son Sam with all their Negroes, mules, and meat, over here to my place. Then if the Yanks come here, I can send them on still farther. That's putting a considerable responsibility on me. She says Sherman's reported to be headed for Macon, and if that is true, we are off the line of march. She also says they are moving along the railroads. And as we are between the railroads, I doubt that they'll visit us."

But rumors kept flying that day and the next, and Mr.

Turner was noticeably uneasy. Friday about noon a note came from Mr. Prudden, the Eatonton postmaster. Though Connecticut born, he had lived in Georgia for so long that here he was, giving his neighbors all the news he could gather about the doings of the "Yankees."

"He says the Yanks have crossed the Ocumulgee," said Mr. Turner, looking over the note in the printing office. "A man told Prudden that they entered Monticello—the county seat of Jasper, you know—at two o'clock this morning. But his postscript was evidently written later. It says 'Indian Spring and Nuting's factory reported burned. 3500 Yankees camped at Social Circle last night.' That means a column is following the Georgia Railroad. Then he adds, 'No Yankees in Monticello at 4 o'clock this morning. This is reliable.'

"That sounds to me," said Mr. Turner, folding the letter slowly, "as if we don't need to worry about our little turnip patch being invaded."

"Nivertheless," said Mr. Wilson when he was gone, "I reserve the right to do me own little private worryin'. Thim Yanks might regard me as a mighty valuable recruit."

Again Turnwold went to bed and slept in a false feeling of security. But on Saturday morning came a note from Dr. Rogers in the west part of the county, which set Mr. Turner on edge again. It read:

> Twenty-five or thirty citizens of Jasper County have just passed, with 75 or 100 negroes on mules. They report the Yankees marching in three columns, one on each railroad, and one through the district between. I advise you to remove all you can, as they are carrying off or destroying everything.

They burnt Monticello last night and Atlanta a few days since.

"I wonder where Sam Reid is," fretted Mr. Turner. "If they've burned Monticello, he ought to be here—if he's coming."

Sam rode in just before dusk, with most of his mother's Negroes, mules and horses, and a wagonload of hams and bacon.

"I had to come, to satisfy Mother," he told Mr. Turner. "I think she's unduly scared. Yes, the Yanks are moving down the railroad, but I don't believe they are coming through the back country. Some other fellows and I did some scouting early this morning, and I can guarantee that there isn't a bluecoat in Putnam County."

Mr. Turner, always eager to be reassured, took heart at this. The mules were stowed away somewhere, and all the cabins in the quarters had guests that night. In the big house, with genial Sam at the table, supper was merry, and the crackling logs in the fireplace made everything seem very cozy and secure. Outside, a slow, cold rain had begun falling.

Joel went to bed early, but was nervous and slept lightly. Somewhere in the night he seemed to hear a voice calling in his dreams. Then suddenly his eyes popped open, and he heard it again—a call of "Hello!" from the road. One did not ride up to a house and knock on the door in those troublous times; one was too apt to receive a bullet from inside.

Joel hurried to a window, but could see nothing in the blackness outside. He heard the murmur of the rain on the roof and in the trees, and the plashing of the gutters, and then heard Mr. Turner call from the front door, "Who's there?"

"A friend," came the reply from the road.

"I suspected it was a Yankee," said Mr. Turner afterward, "but I concluded to face the music." So, "Come in!" he called.

Joel hastily drew on his trousers and a pair of shoes and went to the head of the stairs, where Mrs. Turner, with a cloak around her, was already watching.

They heard horses' hoofs clatter up the house. Then Mr. Turner, who had lighted a candle, opened the door, and two men came in, streaming with water. They wore black felt hats and rubber coats which came down below the tops of their muddy boots, and had the collars turned up around their necks. Were there uniforms under those raincoats? And if so, what color were they?

"Sorry to disturb you, neighbor," said one of the men, "but we're mighty nigh frozen. Can we have a drink of whisky?"

"Certainly," replied Mr. Turner. He went to the dining room, returned with a bottle and two glasses, and poured out a drink for each.

"Couldn't you let us have the bottle?" asked the spokesman. The other man did not speak during the interview. "It's a mighty raw night and we've got to be out in it, not tellin' how long."

Mr. Turner handed over the bottle. There seemed nothing else to do. "Soldiers?" he asked.

"Coupla General Wheeler's scouts," replied the man.

"Then maybe you know where the Yankees are," suggested Mr. Turner.

"That's what we're tryin' to find out. We know they're goin' down the railroad, but are there any in here by the Oconee? That's the question."

They handed their glasses back. "Thanks, Mr.—" His glance at the planter's face was sharp. "This Mr. Turner?"

"Yes," was the reply.

"Well, we know you're a good Confederate. You won't tell the Yankees about us being here."

"Naturally not," said Mr. Turner, with a fine touch of sarcasm as they clumped out. He closed the door and stood by it waiting, until he heard their hoofbeats fade away. Then he called in a guarded tone to the two faces whom he could dimly see at the top of the stairs:

"Is Sam there? Great Scott! Did that fellow sleep through all this? Call him, Joe. We must have a council of war."

He held up his candle and peered at the tall clock in the hall. "Nearly two o'clock," he said. "Strange doings for this time of night."

Sam, sleeping like a log in a rear bedroom, was hard to awaken. He came forth yawning and still complacent. He doubted that the two callers were Union soldiers, and still refused to believe that there were any Yankees in the county.

"Most likely just a couple of Joe Wheeler's scouts, like they said," was his opinion.

"Well, if that chap's Southern accent wasn't a little artificial, then I don't know what I'm talking about," said Mr. Turner.

"That's just what I thought," offered Joel.

Still they couldn't convince Sam, and after a few minutes'

talk, the amazing youth went back to bed and fell asleep again.

But for some reason he awoke at dawn, much more concerned. He dressed, went downstairs, and asked the cook for a cup of coffee and some bread.

"I'm going to scout up the road a piece," he said to Mr. Turner, who, hearing him, had come out to the kitchen and found him standing with bread and coffee cup in his hand.

"Follow the hoof tracks of those fellows and see which way they went," advised Mr. Turner.

"I'll do that." He ran out to the stable for his horse and was off.

In two hours he came tearing back, wild-eyed, spattered with mud even to his hair.

"There's a lot of 'em camped at Park's Bridge," he said, "and the tracks of those two fellows led right back to the camp."

Park's Bridge was only about six miles away. Sam immediately began rounding up his crew of Negroes. They bridled the mules, hitched up the wagon, and away they went, southward, they knew not where, just fleeing before the storm.

Mr. Turner meanwhile shouted for Harbert.

"Get some men and take the horses and mules away out in the swamp and hide them," he told the old man. "The Yankees may be here at any time. Put the horses where they can drink and graze."

It was Sunday, and some of the Negroes had scattered, visiting at neighboring plantations, but Harbert rounded up enough men to take care of the horses.

Joel himself went with them and led his favorite, Butterfly. By tortuous paths which followed the firmer ground and which were known only to two or three of the Negroes, they went far into the swamp toward the Oconee. Joel tethered Butterfly in a canebrake with a long rope, so that she could eat the green cane leaves and drink from a near-by pool.

About noon, Joel, wandering restlessly about the grounds, was at the big gate leading into the road, when two men in blue uniforms with heavy capes came galloping by on fine horses. He stared at them in great curiosity. They were the first Union soldiers he had ever seen; at least they were the first Northern uniforms he had seen. Perhaps last night—

"Hey, boy," called one of them, "how far is it to Eatonton?"

"Nine miles," he replied, and they sped on. They were couriers bearing messages to General Sherman, who was then nearing Eatonton by another road.

Next morning, just as dawn was breaking, Joel was awakened by an unusual stir and tumult. Big four-horse wagons were lumbering along the road, horsemen in blue uniforms were swarming in through the big gates, leaving them open, apparently taking possession. Officers were calling out, "Bring in those cattle!" and "Put those hogs into the wagons." "Sergeant, empty that corn crib." An officer who seemed to be in charge of affairs was talking to Mr. Turner on the porch.

"I regret, sir," said he, "that we shall have to take your cattle and horses and some of your grain. I see you haven't much corn left. Where are your horses?"

"That you will have to find out for yourself," said Mr. Turner.

The officer smiled sarcastically, and said, "We'll do our best." He and Mr. Turner argued for several minutes, the latter evidently restraining his temper with great difficulty. Presently an orderly hurried up, saluted, and said, "Captain, we've found where the horses are. Some of the niggers told us they're hid in the swamp, and they're showin' the way now to Sergeant Ormsby and a squad of men."

"Very good," said the captain, dismissing him. When he looked at Mr. Turner again, he saw that his face was white with baffled rage.

"I'm sorry, Mr. Turner," said the captain. "You see, we need good animals for this long march to the sea. We'll give you some of our discarded horses and mules in their place. A little rest and feed will make them as good as yours."

"You're very kind," said Mr. Turner, with bitter sarcasm. "And on what will I feed them?"

"Oh, there ought to be plenty for them to eat on this big plantation—root crops, fodder, and grass, and you've probably got some corn hidden somewhere."

Old Harbert came hurrying up from the barn. "Dey are gittin' de hosses, Marster," he burst out, "but I didn't tell 'em where dey wuz."

"I know you didn't, Harbert," assured Mr. Turner.

"Hit wuz dat triflin', low-life Zeke," said Harbert, "an' if I kin lay han's on de scoun'el, I'll give him a frailin' dat he'll remember de longest day he lives." He darted a venomous glance at the unwelcome guest's blue uniform, and added, "Does you need any help to gyard de house, Marster?"

"You need not worry, my man," said the captain, "Your family and personal belongings are safe," he added to Mr.

Turner. "General Sherman has given strict orders that there be no looting."

"Then you don't call it looting," said Mr. Turner satirically, "to take all of a man's food and the horses with which he makes a living?"

"In war it is called foraging," replied the captain coldly, "and is considered legitimate, especially in an enemy country. I'll station a guard here to see that nothing is stolen from your home," and he turned away.

Joel wandered about the place and noticed that the soldiers who were doing the foraging were for the most part good-humored, greeting him as "bub" and "Johnny"— "Johnny Reb" was a favorite Northern soldier's nickname for a Southerner. Joel was surprised, for he had gotten the impression that Yankees were all hard, rough, surly men. But there was one of these who was far from genial. Joel saw this man, who had a foreign accent, enter the hat shop, now deserted, and, following him, saw that he was proceeding to load himself with all the hats in the place.

"You leave those hats alone," cried Joel indignantly.

"Shut up, liddle fool!" was the only answer, as the man glowered at him.

"Put those hats down!" cried Joel, standing in the fellow's way. "You haven't any use for them. General Sherman has given orders against looting. I'll tell the captain on you—"

The man, with a sweep of his arm, sent the boy spinning, across the room.

"Yoost for that," said he, "I burn dis place." He swept some papers together, threw some loose wool on them, lighted a match and tossed it into the pile. In another minute the building would have been in flames. But just as he struck the match, a shadow darkened the door and a lieutenant looked in.

"What are you doing, you scoundrel?" he roared. "Throw that rubbish out of the door! Help him get it out, boy!"

"He's trying to steal all our hats," said Joel, as he kicked at the burning paper, the officer helping with his sword. When the blazing mass was well outside, the officer, began to spank the soldier unmercifully with the flat of his sword. Dancing about, screaming "Ow!" and trying to shield himself, the man backed away from the door. Joel laughed till the tears came. It seemed as good as a circus.

"Now get out of here," said the officer, "and if I catch you at this again, I'll have you put in irons."

The soldier hurried off in one direction, and the officer strode away in another without a word. But Joel had scarcely ceased laughing when he saw the horses, among them his beloved Butterfly, being led toward the road by Northern soldiers. Tears stood in his eyes as Butterfly disappeared through the gate into the road, but there was nothing he could do. He just stood with clenched hands and watched her go.

CHAPTER THIRTEEN

The End of a World

THE last wagon had disappeared from the ravaged plantation. Some of the gaunt mules had been un-hitched from them on the spot and left to replace some of the animals taken away. The captain in command of the raid had left a soldier with his gun on guard in front of the mansion to prevent any marauding by other soldiers or "bummers." The road, its mud now deeply cut and churned by hoofs and wagon wheels, was quiet for a few minutes; then a group of mounted officers went clattering by, now in a trot, now in a gallop, their horses' hoofs throwing mud high in the air and spattering their uniforms.

"That's General Slocum and his staff," said the guard. "He commands the left wing of the army now."

Shortly after that, Joel heard a faint noise of singing, and saw that the army was upon them. He ran and climbed up on the fence by the road. A group of officers came riding ahead, and then a long column of men in blue, marching four abreast, though not in perfect order. In fact, dress parade marching would not have been possible on those rough, muddy roads. The whole scene was a dis-appointment to Joel at first. It was not like the glorious pageantry of war as he had imagined it. There were neither bands nor flying banners; all these were being carried in the baggage wagons. There was just a long thick rope of men in faded blue uniforms trailing snakelike over hills and hollows along the winding road; men trudging through mud ankle deep, carrying heavy guns and knapsacks, but singing.

"John Brown's body lies mould'ring in the tomb.
John Brown's body lies mould'ring in the tomb.
John Brown's body lies mould'ring in the tomb.
As we go marching on.

"Glory, glory, hallelujah!
Glory, glory, hallelujah!
Glory, glory, hallelujah!
As we go marching on."

They were singing it raggedly, one company not in tune with another, evidently singing just because they were in good spirits. Then came a break in the line, a major riding at the head of another battalion, and these were not singing, but were in just as happy a frame of mind—laughing and cracking jokes. The small, lonely redheaded figure sitting on the fence attracted their attention, and they tossed many jests at Joel as they went by: "Hello Johnny! Where's your parasol?" for a thin mist was falling again. "Jump down, Johnny, and let me kiss you good-by," called another. Joel could not help grinning back at them, for they were so jovial with it all. But one man with a pale, drawn face staggered out of line and sat down on the wet bank almost at Joel's feet.

Slog, slog, slog, the mud-laden shoes rose and fell.

"Buddy," he gasped in a sharp-voiced drawl—it seemed to Joel that he was talking through his nose—"could you get me a drink of water?"

This was a hated Yankee, but the boy's ideas of Yankees were undergoing a slight change; and, furthermore, his sympathy was aroused by the evidently suffering man. He ran and brought some water in a gourd, the favorite rural drinking vessel in the South in those days.

"Thank ye, son," said the soldier when he had gulped down the water.

"Are you sick?" asked Joel.

"No, jest tired, mostly," was the reply. "I hurt my foot yesterday and it wore me out to march on it." Slowly, every motion showing how tired he was, he took a big cracker— Joel guessed that it was hardtack—out of his knapsack and bit off pieces of it, talking in broken sentences as he chewed.

"Not used to this heavy marchin'. . . . Been indoors all my life—workin' at a bench—clockmaker. . . . Ain't got much taste for war, anyhow. . . . They drafted me a few months ago. . . . Got a wife and four children back in Connecticut."

"Are these all Connecticut soldiers?" asked Joel.

"Oh no. This is the Hundred and Twenty-third New York passin', now. My regiment—Fifth Connecticut—is gone by."

"How will you get back to it?"

"I'll get on a wagon when it comes along and ketch up with the boys tonight, maybe, when they go into camp."

Slog, slog, slog, the thousands of feet plodding through the mud, steadily getting worse as little misty showers fell; still that long dull blue mud-spattered ribbon crawling over the little rise beyond the cornfield. The soldier named some

of the regiments as they went by—"Forty-sixth Pennsylvania... Second Massachusetts... Thirteenth New Jersey."
... Again the jokes. "Hey soldier," called someone in the ranks to the straggler, "has Johnny on the fence took you prisoner?" During an interval between divisions, another group of mounted officers came in sight, spurring along rapidly. The Connecticut soldier struggled to his feet and stood at attention.

"General Alph Williams, new commander of the Twentieth Corps and his staff," said he out of the corner of his mouth to Joel. "He's the feller with the big, forked beard and long mustache."

"Is all this the Twentieth Corps?" asked Joel, when the man had sat down again.

"Yes, but you won't see more'n half of it. The other part is goin' by another road."

"Is it all from the Eastern states?"

"Oh no, we've got regiments from Ohio, Indiana, Illinois, and le's see—one from Michigan."

"How many men are in the corps?" was Joel's next question.

"About 14,000, as I ricollect," said the man.

Slog, slog, slog, the mud-laden shoes rose and fell, the moving thicket of guns bobbed up and down with them as Joel pondered all this. War had lost its glitter for him, but the spectacle was beginning to have a frightening grandeur which he hadn't seen in it before. Never before had he had the faintest realization of what a thousand men, five thousand men meant. There seemed to be no end to the marching column. He was beginning to be awed and frightened by the immensity and power which he saw there.

Presently, at the end of a division, several wagons came

along, and the Connecticut man rose and hobbled toward the road.

"Good-by, buddy," he said over his shoulder. "Thanks for the drink. Come and see me." He climbed on the tail-gate of one of the wagons while the grinning driver was calling to Joel, "Run and git your trunk, Johnny, and git aboard!"

Another division commander and his staff and then more infantry, most of them good-natured, unheeding the sticky red clay which sucked at their feet and weighted their shoes, making marching doubly hard. Still they found the small, lone, freckle-faced figure on the fence pleasantly humorous.

"Where's your regiment, Johnny?" "He's a bush-whacker, boys; if he so much as bats his eye, I'm goin' to dodge." "If there was another one of 'em settin' on t'other side of the road, I'd say we was surrounded."

Joel, tired now and then of watching the moving column, went away when the rain became a little heavier, but was always drawn back to the road again after a while by an irresistible fascination. He couldn't help thinking of that gentle Connecticut clockmaker who didn't want to fight. Would he get back alive to his wife and children? The spectacle was beginning to have new meaning for Joel. These men didn't look any different from Georgians. Their faces were much like those of home folks. Take the blue uniform off them and you wouldn't know the difference. And probably they all or nearly all had people back there in those Northern states who loved them, and were praying for their safe return. That day was destined to play an important part in this thoughtful boy's life. It had an influence on his writing years afterward.

Late in the afternoon he saw the end of the infantry column; then came strings of horses and cows seized from other farms, and a portion of the vast wagon train of the army, many of the wagons, to his astonishment, carrying big flat-bottomed boats—one boat to each wagon. Joel had read of pontoon bridges, but he had supposed that the pontoons were made at the water's edge when the soldiers came to a stream. But this army, expecting to find bridges destroyed in its path, and not wishing to be bothered with ferrying, carried its own bridges of boats with it.

"De governor and de legislature has all run away f'm Milledgeville," was Harbert's news, when he went back to the house again.

So there was no longer a state government in Georgia! A stunned silence reigned over Turnwold that night. Joel thought often of those soldiers going into camp a few miles away on the muddy ground, among wet grass and under-brush, trying to start fires with sodden wood, perhaps some of them sleeping, or trying to sleep, without tents in the cold drizzling rain. No, there was no longer any glamour in war for him.

Next day, work on the plantation was almost at a stand-still. Mr. Turner, haggard and tired, was trying to re-organize his little community. More than half his Negroes were gone, they had followed the Federal army, as did thousands of others in Georgia, expecting to be cared for and to have a happy life without work. Harbert, Uncle George, and most of the older ones were still faithful, but the younger ones, especially those who worked in the fields and had not been on familiar terms with the master had vanished, and numerous cabins were vacant.

"It's lucky for me," sighed Mr. Turner. "Sherman will

have to feed them, if they're fed at all. I don't know how I could have done it this winter, after this raid." He paused for a moment, staring at the wall, and said, "It looks like the beginning of the end, Joel."

Work on *The Countryman* was forgotten that week. As Joel stood at the big gate next morning looking northward along the road, peopling it again in his mind with the thousands of men he had seen marching over it yesterday, he thought he saw something move in a fence corner a hundred yards away. Looking more keenly, he was sure there was a human being there. He walked toward it, and saw that it was an old colored woman, thinly clad, sitting on a stone, shivering and moaning. Beyond her, in the fence corner, lay an aged Negro man, his shoulders covered by a ragged shawl.

"Who is that lying there, Auntie?" asked Joel.

"My ol' man, suh."

"What is the matter with him."

"He dead, suh," she replied simply. "But bless God, he died free."

There was a catch in Joel's throat for a moment. Then he asked, "Where did you come from?"

"F'm Morgan County, little mahster. We was followin' Giner'l Sherman to freedom, but my ol' man, he couldn't go any furder."

She burst into sobs, and rocked to and fro.

"I'll bring some help, Auntie," said Joel, and sped away. Soon he returned, bringing Harbert and three other men. Gently they carried the body of the old slave, who had found his freedom, back to the quarters. They had to carry his wife also, for she was in a state of exhaustion. Next day there was a funeral service, with one of the Negroes who was a lay preacher officiating, and the elderly stranger was buried in the little plantation cemetery.

His wife had been put to bed in one of the cabins deserted by a family who had followed the army. There the Turners and the colored people tended her carefully, though it was evident that she had not long to live. Joel visited her frequently, and she invoked many blessings upon the "little mahster" who had been so kind to her. Within a few weeks, she went, quite contentedly, to join her "ol' man" in eternal freedom.

In the issue of *The Countryman* for the week following the passage of the army, Mr. Turner remarked that during the past week he had been "entertaining some gentlemen from the United States of North America, including a few from Europe." There would be quite an interesting story to tell of the invasion, he said, but "we deem it prudent to omit it for the present. The truth is, we don't know just now whether we are a subject of Joe Brown, Gov. Logan, Jeff Davis, old Abe or the King of Dahomey."

Thereafter, the paper appeared in smaller size. Of course, no new subscribers appeared, and it could not be profitable. The plantation struggled through the latter part of that winter somehow, though food for humans and the few animals left became painfully scarce. Even at that, Turnwold was more fortunate than some other country places where the buildings had been burned and only devastation left.

In May 1865, Mr. Turner wrote an editorial, saying that he had just heard of the surrender of the main Confederate armies to the Union generals, Grant and Sherman, that henceforth he would publish the paper in greatly reduced size and would say nothing about politics until he learned how much he would be permitted to say.

"I suppose I may as well tell you, Harbert," he said when the old man came to him for orders about some matter, "that you people are all free."

Harbert peered into his face with something of consternation in his eyes. "You ain't goin' to send us away, is you, Marster?" he asked.

"Not if you don't want to go," replied Mr. Turner. "You may stay as long as we can find something to eat on the place. How long that will be I don't know."

So *The Countryman* became just a little leaflet, scarcely larger than a book page. Mr. Turner calmly announced his acceptance of the new regime: "Reunion—Henceforth we desire to know no North, no South, no East, no West, but one common country." Nevertheless, a harsh Federal general named Wilson, who was in military control of Georgia at the time, seized him and kept him for several weeks in prison at Macon on the charge of "disloyal utterances." The effect of such injustice upon a proud soul like Mr. Turner was calamitous. He never quite recovered his spirit thereafter.

Of course, *The Countryman* was suspended while he was in prison, and for several weeks after he was freed. When he began issuing it again, he showed a flash of his old humor. The paper's motto formerly had been "Independent in everything, neutral in nothing." Now he changed it to "Independent in nothing, neutral in everything."

Joel had remained at Turnwold all this time, helping to look after the farm work. When the paper resumed publi-

"You ain't goin' to send us away, is you, Marster?" he asked.

cation, he went back to his old job, though there was not much to do. Mr. Turner, in his melancholy, found some comfort in the belief that he was coaching one of the future great writers of the South. Once Louise Prudden, Joel's former little seatmate, now a pretty girl of sixteen who was showing promise as a writer, came to visit at Turnwold. With one hand upon her shoulder and the other on Joel's, Mr. Turner said, "You two will do the writing for the South which I will be unable to do."

Smiling, looking at her old playmate, Louise asked, "What are you going to write about, Joe?"

The conversation was becoming too emotional for Joel, and as usual at such times, he struck back at it with a piece of nonsense. Blushing furiously, he muttered, "B-bumble-bees and jaybirds."

He was nearer right than he knew.

Through another winter the little paper dragged along. Turnwold took care, not only of its own Negroes but of several who had drifted in from other plantations, where all the buildings had been burned and the masters fled. One of Mr. Turner's last editorials shows a spirit far in advance of many of those around him:

If the negro is forced upon us as a citizen, we go for educating him, inducing him to accumulate property and to do other things which make a good citizen. In his attempts at elevating himself he should receive all the aid and encouragement in the power of our people to give him.

How greatly Joel Harris's thought and life were influenced by this kindly slave owner and gentleman, no one can tell. But the end of their pleasant association was drawing near. Mr. Turner came into the shop one day, and said, "I'm sorry to tell you, Joel, that we can't go on. I haven't the money to buy any more paper and ink."

Sadly, Joel set the type and ran off the sheets for the last time. On the margin of the copy which he kept all his life, he wrote:

> This is the *very last* number of *The Countryman* ever issued. I mean this is the last paper printed; and it **was** printed by my hand May 9, 1866. It was established March 4, 1862, having lived four years, two months and four days.
>
> J. C. HARRIS

When they had prepared the few copies for mailing, Mr. Turner looked around the shop sadly. "There'll be no more happy days here at Turnwold, such as we've known in the past. For me the end of the world has come. But you are young and talented. Life is all before you. There will be a place for you somewhere, and my best wishes go with you. It's been a great pleasure to have you here, Joel, and you have been a loyal and able employee and friend. I hope I have helped you a little toward the career of which I can see you're dreaming."

"Y-you have, sir!" stammered Joel. "M-more than I can ever tell you."

It was hard to say good-by to this kind family, to the loyal black friends, and to the little shop, the woods, and fields where he had been so happy for four years. It was agony to Joel because he could not express in words his gratitude to them all, and his sorrow in parting. But he turned his back upon them at last and started on his walk to Eatonton. He was almost penniless. Mr. Turner had been able to pay him little since the end of the war, and all that he had earned before that had, of course, been paid to him in Confederate money, which was now not worth the paper it was printed upon. But even so, it was as his employer had said: He was the more fortunate of the two. The war ruined Mr. Turner, as it did many another Southern planter, and he died only two years later, brokenhearted and in poverty.

As for Joel, those years at Turnwold formed one of the most important periods of his life. There he found material for many of the stories which brought him fame. There he found encouragement for his ambition and some knowledge of the practical side of publishing. There he may be said, in four years, to have grown from boyhood to manhood. There he really began his literary career.

CHAPTER FOURTEEN

One Foot on the Ladder

LONG before he left Turnwold, Joel had begun to think of venturing into the world outside the plantation. Less than two years after he began work there, he wrote to a former Eatonton friend, a little older than himself, who had a place in a newspaper shop down at Columbus, Georgia, asking if there was a chance of his finding work with that paper. It may seem odd to think of a boy of fifteen expecting to take a man's place in a printing shop, but so many of the men in the South had been drawn into the armies that a great deal of their usual work at home was being done by boys and old men. Furthermore, it must be admitted that by this time Joel could set type just about as well as any man in the business.

The friend in Columbus wrote, "I should be delighted if you could come, as I am bored to death with the society with which I am compelled to associate. The boys in the office are, with a few exceptions, stupid wooden-heads. Now, as to work; I can only say that I have tried in all the offices, and there is no empty case—all full at present. . . . You can get a 'sit' in Macon, no doubt, but you will have to work, work, all the time, day and night, and you will soon get tired of it."

This letter was such a damper that Joel, still loath to venture into strange scenes, did nothing more until *The Countryman* ceased to exist. Then he went home and began writing letters here and there asking for work. He took his friend's advice and centered his attack on Macon, one of the leading cities of the state. Aided by strong recommendations from Mr. Turner and men in his home town, he quickly found a place in the composing room of the *Macon Telegram*. He was only seventeen.

The managing editor must have wondered, when the freckled, undersized boy weighing less than a hundred pounds stood before him, blushing and stammering, whether he had done wisely in taking on such a youngster; and yet young Harris's letters had been written in such faultless English and sounded so intelligent—he took them out again and looked them over to be sure he was not mistaken. Perhaps someone else had written them for him. Anyhow, his recommendations were excellent. Well, it would be only fair to give the boy a chance and see how genuine he was.

Joel's first work was that of taking proofs and helping the foreman. He was quiet, having little to say to anybody at first, and he studied carefully every detail of the making of what seemed to him this great and important city newspaper with a press operated by steam. In his spare time, both in and out of working hours, he was reading and writing.

Soon he was given a chance to set type.

"That cub will do," said the old foreman, bringing some proof sheets of his work to Harry Neville, the city editor. "He's fast and he's accurate. Here are a couple of galleys he's set. Look 'em over."

"Well, there's a lot of truth in the old saying that you can't tell by looking at a frog how far he can jump," said Mr. Neville, when he had glanced over the proofs. "What seems still more incredible is that this schoolboy, not dry behind the ears yet, is supposed to have written a lot of excellent things in *The Countryman*—you remember the paper, Ed—some of them as much as two years ago when he was still more of an infant than he is now. It gets me!"

It wasn't long before Mr. Neville began giving Joel the task of writing small items for the paper. He would pick out some event which he thought well suited to the boy's style and ask him to write it up. In those days, business concerns sometimes secured free puffs in the paper by giving a present to the editor or a treat to the whole staff of employees, which would bring out an item something like this:

"Mr. Liebman, the well-known Eighth Street baker, placed on our table yesterday a large and handsome fruit cake which proved to be one of the finest delicacies of the sort that we ever stuck a tooth into. The staff cleaned it up in short order, much to the editor's regret, and all agreed that it could not be surpassed. Mr. Liebman's goods are always of this high quality, and our lady readers are advised to let him do their baking for them instead of spending hours over a hot stove at home."

Some items of this sort were assigned to Joel, and he wrote them in such an unusual and lively manner that they attracted much attention. In his reports of other events, he now began to show evidences of the humor which was to be a chief characteristic of all his mature writing.

Because of his greenness and good humor, the other workmen in the office at first imposed upon him, putting more work upon him than was his due. But he took it so good naturedly and was so likable that they ceased to do this after a while, and all became fond of him. Because of the color of his hair, the office nickname for him was "Pink-Top"; but the jest grew to be an affectionate one.

As he became better acquainted with his work, and acquired some closer friendships on the staff, he relaxed and spent some time with them in his evening hours. Perhaps his best chum was a young man not much older than himself named Bridges Smith, who years later studied law and became a judge. This gentleman used to laugh over the time when Joel "completed his trade," as the saying was, by joining the local typographical union. The ceremony took place on a Sunday afternoon in a little brick engine house, the home of a volunteer fire company known as Young America No. 3, where the union met.

To join the union, it was necessary to repeat the words of an obligation. Joel had it all memorized, but when the time came, he was seized with such a panic that he was unable to say a word. The silence grew painful, and finally Bridges Smith, amused but pitying his friend's embarrassment, said, "Mr. President, Mr. Harris stutters."

"Well, I guess we will have to take the will for the deed," said the president, after another few moments' hesitation, and so Joel joined the union without promising loyalty, as prescribed by the by-laws.

All the time Joel was writing articles, poems, and, sometimes, stories for Southern magazines, for most of which he still received no pay. Among the magazines to which he contributed was the *Crescent Monthly,* published in New Orleans. Its editor was that same Captain Flash, the former Macon journalist whose poems and prose style Joel had admired so much, and about whom he had written in *The Countryman*. Captain Flash was naturally much pleased by Joel's praise, and it was through him that an offer came —when Joel had been in Macon not yet four months—of a place as secretary to Mr. William Evelyn, owner of the magazine.

Joel was almost in consternation at the thought of what the offer meant. New Orleans was so far away. . . . It was such a big city. . . . He would have to go among strangers, make acquaintances all over again. . . . The problem was, for two or three days, a nightmare to him, and in despair of solving it himself, he finally decided to lay it before Mr. Neville. He went into the editor's office red and flustered, handed him the letter, and said, "M-Mister Neville, th-this letter came for me Monday. I d-didn't ask for a job there. I don't know how they happened to ask me."

Mr. Neville was pretty well acquainted with Joel's character by that time. He read the letter through, and asked, "Well, what do you think of it, Joe?"

"I don't know what to think," was the reply. "I came to ask your advice."

The editor hesitated a moment. "It's a bigger thing than we can offer you, Joe," he finally said slowly. "More salary, perhaps a bigger chance for promotion. And New Orleans is a wonderful city. Many cultures there—Anglo-Saxon, French, Spanish; you'll see and hear things which will be of great value to you. I know your ambition. You want to be an author. On a magazine you will have a better chance to cultivate your talent as it should be cultivated than on a newspaper."

He felt silent so long that Joel finally asked, "Then you advise me to accept?"

His eyes were round with wonder.

Lordly steamboats with their gold-braided officers.

"Giving advice in a case like this is dangerous business," said Mr. Neville. "All I can say is this, Joe: If I were only seventeen and in your shoes, I would accept the offer without hesitation."

Yet Joel hesitated for at least two days more before writing his letter of acceptance. He left Macon with regret for he had made friends there, and he liked his employers. Many years later, in a letter to one of his children, who was visiting in that hospitable city, with the broad tree-shaded streets, he said, "You can't tell me anything about Macon. I once lived there and liked it very much. The people are fine. . . ."

Now for the first time in his life he ventured outside the familiar atmosphere of Georgia, and for weeks on end as he moved about New Orleans his eyes were round with wonder. A great, lazy river, which seemed not to move at all, lordly steamboats with their gold-braided officers and aristocratic passengers, ocean vessels which had come up the mighty stream one hundred miles from the sea, bustling docks littered with baled cotton and coffee and sugar and a thousand other things, the vast sullen swamps, the strange bird and animal life, the long moss trailing from the trees like funereal decorations—why, here he seemed to be in a foreign country! The narrow, cobbled streets with their lovely romantic names—Bienville, Iberville, Baronne (where his own office was), Dryades, Melpomene, Clio . . . The mansions in some quarters of town with lacy ironwork over the porches, yards full of flowering trees, shrubs and vines, and the air heavy with the scent of bloom, the strange foods—lobster, crab, shrimp, crawfish . . . The soft Creole dialect, even Negroes talking French. . . . The old colored woman with her basket of vegetables on her way from market, who dropped on her knees on the stone floor just inside the door of St. Louis Cathedral and said her little morning prayer . . . The stall keeper in the old French market, shoveling up live crawfish with a scoop like the grocer at home used for sugar, pouring them into a paper bag on the scales, and the woman customer going off with them, audibly scuffling and scratching inside the bag— It was all as fascinating as a play. There was a young newspaper reporter named George W. Cable, working in the city at the time, who was keenly alive to its charm, and who later wrote it into some fine short stories and novels.

But Joel did not give all his spare moments to sight-seeing. He spent much time outside office hours in writing paragraphs and unsigned articles for his employer's magazine, and also for the New Orleans papers.

"You'll have to be careful what you write for these papers, Joe," grinned Captain Flash, when he heard of this sideline, "or you'll have somebody taking a pot shot at you on the street or an elegant gentleman walking in here one morning with a challenge for you. These fire-eating editors down here crave your blood if you so much as bat an eyelash crooked. We'd hate to see you toted home plumb full of holes or all messed up with a bowie knife."

Truly enough, the brawls and duels in which the editors there were involved seemed too numerous for comfort, and Joel was careful to write nothing which would offend these touchy citizens. Many of his productions were romantic little poems. He was ashamed of most of them when he grew older, and called them doggerel. One of them which is known to be his work was "The Sea Wind," written for the *New Orleans Times*. It began:

O sweet south wind! O soft south wind!
  O wind from off the sea!
When you blow to the inland ports of home
  Kiss my love for me.

Odd that a youth who had never had a love affair should write so fervently of love!

Joel was very useful to his employer and editor. He is said to have written all but one of a series of lectures on English literature which Mr. Evelyn, the proprietor, delivered before a girls' school in New Orleans. But after all, New Orleans was never home to Joel. It was too foreign, too different from the rustic Georgia environment in which he had grown up and which he ever afterward preferred to all others. He tasted the rare food in the famous French restaurants of the old Creole city, but let others praise them as they would, he preferred corn bread and buttermilk, fried chicken, ham, and collards.

He was homesick, too, for the red clay banks, homely living and crisper winters of Georgia, and fate helped him to get back there. The *Crescent Monthly,* never prosperous, died when he had been in its office less than a year, and back he came in May 1867, "nursing a novel in his brain," as he said, to spend a little while with his mother in Eatonton, "ruralizing in the places where grain grows and birds sing."

CHAPTER FIFTEEN

Joel Builds a Reputation

BUT Joel couldn't afford to be without a salary long, so after a very brief vacation, he began looking for a place again. He was going into Macon on a train one day, with his flabby carpetbag in his hand, hoping to find a composing-room job again, when he saw on the platform of one of the coaches a familiar face—none other than that of Jim Harrison, who had worked for a time in *The Countryman* office. Jim was a few years older than Joel, and to Joel he was always "Mr. Harrison." He looked in every direction but the right one, until just as the train was cranking to a stop, his glance fell upon Joel. He stared for a moment, then his face lighted up with recognition.

"Joe Harris," he exclaimed, reaching for the boy's hand, "is it really you?"

"Y-yes sir," stammered Joel, blushing as usual.

"What do you mean by that 'sir'? Well, well, how you've changed since I saw you last! How many years has it been? Three? Four? I've been hearing of your career. Where are you working now? Still in New Orleans?"

"No," said Joel. "The magazine collapsed. I'm out of a job now."

"Is that so?" They were climbing down the steps to the station platform. "Listen! Come over here where we can talk." Jim dragged him by the arm to a quiet corner. "You may be the very man I'm looking for. I've bought the newspaper up at Forsyth, in Monroe County, just northwest of here. It's called the *Monroe Advertiser*. I always wanted to publish a newspaper. Now I have to have somebody to run the shop. You could do that—and some of the writing, too. Would you consider such a place?"

"Why, yes, I might," said Joel.

"Now, as to wages." Harrison hesitated a moment. "A country newspaper, you know, can't pay fancy salaries. But I'll tell you what I'll do. I'm married now—finest little wife you ever saw, Joe—and I'll give you board and lodging in my home as part pay. Add to that—well, say seven dollars a week in cash. Does that sound all right?"

Joel hesitated. To go and live in a strange home again, with a young woman fussing around him, having to eat at the table with her. . . .

Jim Harrison misunderstood his hesitation. "Well, make it eight dollars."

"Oh, that's all right!" gasped Joel. And thus at eighteen he became well-nigh the mainstay of a country newspaper. Long afterward, he humorously described his job thus:

"I set all the type, pulled the press, kept the books, swept the floor, and wrapped the papers for mailing; my mechanical, accounting, and menial duties being concealed from the vulgar hilarity of the world outside of Forsyth by the honorable and impressive title of Editor."

Jim Harrison had ideas. The *Monroe Advertiser* was one of the first newspapers in the county to have a local department; that is, columns of personal items about the little everyday doings of citizens of the town and surrounding country. Up to that time newspapers thought they were called upon only to record important political news, preferably about the state and nation, with some items describing great disasters and other momentous or curious happenings in various parts of the world—all this clipped from other papers, of course. Local news was being given much more space by the time Joel went into the *Advertiser* office, but still there was no column in which the little visits and travels and sicknesses and accidents of ordinary folk were recorded. To publish material like this would have, up to that time, been considered a sort of yellow journalism.

"Other people beside politicians have a right to have their names in the paper, Joel," said his employer. "I think they'll be interested in seeing their own names and those of their neighbors in print, and I think it will win a lot of new readers for us."

So the *Advertiser* began carrying a column of items such as everyone who reads a country newspaper sees to this day:

Ed Simpson has gone back to college at Athens.

Mr. John A. Timmins was in Macon on business yesterday.

Miss Hattie Gates of Dames Ferry is visiting Miss Willie Toland.

Mr. Azariah Dickey of the Towaliga neighborhood was in town yesterday, shopping. He says the crops look good out his way.

Mr. Henry Huskins had the misfortune to have his right kneecap broken Thursday by the kick of a horse. He is resting comfortably at this writing.

This department greatly increased the *Advertiser's* circulation, but editor and proprietor must have had to do considerable "leg work," as the reporters say, to gather the material. Joel also wrote paragraphs, commenting on local, state, and national news, and here he began to display the rich fund of humor which soon earned him a wide reputation. The terse, snappy paragraphs were copied into other papers far and wide. The *Atlanta Constitution* published a string of them at intervals under the heading of "Harrisoniana," but as time went on other editors learned who was really responsible for them, and then and there Joel's reputation as a journalistic wit was born.

All this work and the increased circulation made the office so busy that within a few months Mr. Harrison said, "Joe, I'm going to take on an apprentice to help you in the shop. There's a farmer boy named Turner Manry that wants to learn the trade. Of course, I can give him only his board and clothes at first. You don't mind his rooming with you, do you?"

"N-no," said Joel slowly. He did mind; he dreaded it. But it would have done no good to say so.

In later life, Turner Manry moved to Louisiana and became a member of the state legislature. But his appearance gave no promise of such a future on that day when he came walking in from his father's farm, seven miles out in the country, a gawky youth of seventeen carrying all his belongings in a flabby carpetbag.

His new boss took him into the shop—where he saw the first type case and printing press that he had ever laid eyes on—and introduced him to Joel, who shook hands and mumbled something. Turner's first impression of him was that "he had the reddest hair I ever saw, and had less to say than anyone I had ever met."

But as they became better acquainted, Joel thawed, and grew quite talkative with the new helper. Turner was tremendously awed by him, and never called him anything but "Mr. Harris." He looked on with amazement as Joel composed paragraphs and even long articles, standing at the case. One which he long remembered, "A Fox Hunt in Georgia," describing one of those dear old days at Turn-wold, was a column and a half in length.

"I don't see how you do it, Mr. Harris," he said over and over again.

Manry first took on the "devil's" work, then learned to read proofs and then to set type. Jobs were strenuous in the *Advertiser* office—ten or twelve hours a day, and every week, just before the paper came out, they had to work evenings. But Turner could not remember that Joel ever took an hour off during the more than two years of their association. After some further years of experience in the business, he declared that Joel was the best pressman he ever saw, and that as a writer he could say more in ten lines than many editors could say in a column.

Newspapers exchanged copies with one another then, and magazines sent copies gratis to newspaper offices in order to get an occasional free notice. All the best magazines, including *Blackwood's,* the *Living Age, Harper's, Appleton's,* and others came to the *Advertiser's* office, and Joel, a voracious reader, contrived to absorb the most of their contents—another amazing thing to young Manry. He was deeply absorbed in Dickens's last work, *The Mystery of Edwin Drood,* as it came out in monthly installments, and was greatly shocked when the novelist's sudden death ended the story in the middle of its course.

"What a loss to literature!" he mourned. "What a loss to the world! And he was writing one of his best stories. . . . I wonder if he told anyone how it was to come out."

"Turner," he said to his young helper, "you don't read enough. You don't read any books."

"Well, I never seem to find time," defended Manry sheepishly. "I never seem to get around to it."

"You just haven't formed a reading habit," said his mentor.

"Joe's right," said their employer, who was present. "You can't get anywhere in journalism, Turner, unless you have done some reading. Dr. Jayne, the druggist, has a little circulating library. Why don't you join it?"

"I'll do that, sir," promised Manry, always ready to take the advice of those two great men. "You tell me what books to pick out, Mr. Harris."

"Here's one for you to start on," said Joel that afternoon, handing the youth a copy of *A Tale of Two Cities*. "A great story of the French revolution by Dickens. I want you to read it carefully—you'll enjoy it, too—and tell me what you think of it. Criticize it if you think it has any weak points."

Turner read it, and said, "That sure was an interesting book, Mr. Harris. I'd heard a lot about that French revolution, but I never realized what it was like before."

"Well, now would be a good time to discover what it was all about," said Joel. He found a history of France, not too heavy, and gave that to his young pupil to read. And so he continued his cultivation in literary taste in the young man, which Manry remembered gratefully for the rest of his life. He remembered also how thoughtful Joel was toward everyone, especially those in humbler positions. Knowing that Manry received no salary, he would frequently stand treat, especially on hot summer days, when a watermelon or a glass of soda would be particularly refreshing.

It was at Forsyth that Joel had his first taste of what seemed real literary fame. A man named Davidson was compiling a work which he called *Living Writers of the*

South, and he asked the young printer-scribe to prepare the index for it. He also sought Mr. Harris's opinion as to the disputed authorship of the famous Civil War poem beginning, "All quiet along the Potomac tonight." A Southern man named Fontaine was claiming the authorship, although the poem, so far as known, had first appeared in *Harper's Weekly* over the initials of a New York woman. Joel made a long and serious investigation, and decided in favor of the New Yorker.

Living Writers of the South contained, among others, a sketch—Joel blushed and wriggled with modesty when he looked at it, even in solitude—of none other than Mr. J. Chandler Harris himself. It contained at least one glaring error, namely the statement that Mr. Harris was studying law.

Mrs. Harrison was very kind to the two young men, and she and her sister-in-law, Mrs. Starke, who paid her some long visits during Joel's stay in Forsyth, did all they could to overcome his agonizing bashfulness. When he first arrived, he sat completely tongue-tied at the table during meals, and escaped as soon afterward as possible. He was morbidly conscious of his awkwardness, and he had been teased so much about his red hair and freckles that he thought himself much more unattractive to other people than he really was. Mrs. Harrison and Mrs. Starke were thoughtful and tactful, and he presently began to be more at ease with them.

But the person who really brought him out of his shell was Mrs. Starke's tiny daughter, Nora Belle, who took to him at once, and was too young to notice his timidity. She climbed into his lap and put her arms around his neck, and his heart opened up to her as it seldom did to anyone. All his life he fell an easy captive to any child, and the children in turn loved him. Even after he left Forsyth, Joel sent gifts to Nora Belle, and once he wrote a little poem to her.

Mr. Harrison's younger, unmarried sister Nora also became an acquaintance of Joel's, but he was never quite at his ease with her. One winter Sunday afternoon they were walking together—and how *that* happened, it is hard to understand--while the sun was setting, redly and gloriously, amid tattered clouds edged with gold.

"Oh, isn't it lovely! Isn't it wonderful!" exclaimed Miss Nora, ecstatically. "It creates inexpressible thoughts in my soul. What do you think of it, Mr. Harris?" She was hoping to evoke some beautiful poetic expression from the young genius. But he was repelled as usual by what he considered "gush," and just stammered:

"R-rem-minds me of a d-dish of scrambled eggs."

Miss Nora was disgusted with him. Apparently he never stood so high in her estimation afterward.

His salary rose while he was in Forsyth, until he was receiving forty dollars a month plus his board and lodging. He sent money to his mother, and her life began to be much easier than it had been for years past. And he also began to gratify modestly a young man's natural liking for nice clothes. His and Turner's room at the Harrisons' house contained little beside the bed, a pine table, two chairs, and Joel's trunk. But the trunk had in it several white shirts with pleated bosoms and some fine English socks. He was particular about his clothes—though some people declared that they didn't fit—and took good care of them.

When once Joel got acquainted, he was a good talker,

Joel made one flying leap through the window.

and might even be lively and full of jokes. The talk at the Harrisons' dining table was well worth hearing, so Turner Manry thought, and Joel and some of the young men of the town had a club called "Company Two," of which he was one of the leading spirits.

But his timidity, actually a horror of meeting strangers, continued. Twice after he left Forsyth he visited Mrs. Starke and her husband at their home in Milledgeville. Once, while they were sitting in the parlor with a close friend or two, some people who were strangers to Joel were seen approaching the house.

He became red and nervous at once. There was only one exit from the parlor, and that was through the hall, which was now blocked by the incoming callers. Mrs. Starke, laughing, whispered, "You are cornered now! You can't get away."

But he did! The house was built in a favorite old Southern fashion, rather high off the ground, so that the window sills were seven or eight feet in the air. Nevertheless, Joel made one flying leap through a window into the yard and vanished for the afternoon.

He added nothing to his stock of Negro folklore while he was in Forsyth, but he did find something which was destined to become immortal. There was an old Negro in the town who, since he was made free, had earned his living by working in the gardens of the townsfolk, and the name of this old man was Remus! Of course, everybody called him Uncle Remus. The name struck Joel as amusing, and when, a few years later, he began writing the stories which brought him fame, he represented them as being told by a kindly old plantation Negro to whom he gave the name of the obscure gardener in Forsyth.

The news finally spread among other editorial offices in Georgia that the editing and all the best writing on the *Monroe Advertiser* was being done by a redheaded youngster named Harris who never had a word to say for himself. The result was that when Joel had been there about three years, he received a letter one morning which fairly struck him dumb with astonishment. He read it through a second time, and still it seemed almost incredible. As usual, he went directly to his employer.

"M-Mr. Harrison," he blurted out, "the *S-Savannah N-News* has offered me forty dollars a week."

Mr. Harrison stared at him in amazement. Forty dollars a week was a high salary for any newspaper man in those days, let alone a kid not yet twenty-two.

"Here's the l-letter," said Joel, handing it to him.

Mr. Harrison read it through.

"Well, I won't pretend that I wasn't expecting something of this kind," he said, slowly. "You've made a reputation, Joel, and I couldn't expect you to stay in Forsyth forever. It will be impossible to fill your place, but I'll have to do the best I can."

CHAPTER SIXTEEN

Savannah Humorist

SAVANNAH! Another beautiful, elderly Southern city, with broad, tree-shaded streets, gracious old mansions, great live-oaks trailing long streamers of moss, the scent of magnolia and gardenia blooms, forts and scars of Civil War and revolution, memories of colonial days long before that, even back to the time of the founder, Oglethorpe. But it had something of Georgia in it, and it was therefore more like home to Joel than New Orleans had been.

It was a slow-moving, easy-going city in those days. Joel used to tell how he once ran to catch a street car when he first went there, which was such a startling thing to do that people on the car stared at him in amazement, and one old lady whispered to another, "If you think he's crazy, we'll get off." But perhaps that was just one of Joel's jokes after he moved to Atlanta. Atlanta loved to tease prim, touchy old Savannah.

Joel approached the place with his usual dread of meeting new associates and acquaintances. He chuckled in middle life, and remarked that with a salary of forty dollars a week assured him, he felt like "the biggest man in the world." But that feeling was all inside him; none of it appeared in his demeanor.

He had raised a mustache by this time, so that he did not look quite so boyish. But when Colonel Estill, the proprietor of the *News,* took him up to the editorial room to introduce him to Colonel Thompson, the editor, and the rest of the staff, one of the reporters said, "We thought at the time that he was the greenest, gawkiest-looking specimen of humanity our eyes had ever rested upon."

After Colonel Estill and Joel had left the room, the others turned to Colonel Thompson and bombarded him with jokes about the new paragrapher.

"What is that critter that Colonel Estill has found?" asked one. "Is it human or what?"

"How did the colonel catch him—in a fishtrap or a net?" wisecracked another.

Colonel Thompson smiled comfortably. "Fact of the matter is, boys, that I myself am responsible for bringing him here. He is the wittiest paragrapher in Georgia. He will rather surprise you, if I'm not mistaken."

The fact that Thompson himself was a humorist explains why he was so strongly drawn to young Harris. Two volumes entitled *Major Jones's Courtship* and *Major Jones's Travels,* written before Joel was born, and bearing the name of W. T. Thompson on the title page, are still valued as humorous pictures of Southern village and backwoods life before the Civil War.

Any newcomer to a newspaper staff was doomed to suffer some unmerciful teasing. But that evening, when Joel's manuscript—written in pencil, as all newspaper copy was then and for long afterward—began to come to the composing room, the printers said to one another, "Say, that new fellow has had some writing lessons, anyhow. You can read every word of his stuff—clear as print!"

This was an unusual blessing, for many editors and reporters, in their haste, wrote very badly. The great editor, Horace Greeley, wrote such atrocious script that hardly anybody could read it.

Manuscript for the *News* was sent into the composing room as fast as it was written and impaled on a hook on the wall. After Joel came, the printers would watch for his copy. When sheets written by others came in, the printers would pretend to be busy at something else. But when they saw from a distance a fresh sheet on the hook with that clear, even copybook writing of the new man, there was a rush for it, and the fellow who captured it was happy.

The staff found, as Colonel Thompson had predicted, that Joel's work was superior in journalistic quality, too. His particular job was the creation of snappy paragraphs of the sort which had made his reputation at Forsyth; comment, usually humorous, sometimes sharply satirical, upon local, state, or national happenings or characters. Georgia's statesmen and politicans came in for a deal of, usually good-natured, teasing, as did certain institutions of which this or that community was proud—Augusta's canal project and the State-owned railroad, for example. He was amused at the rapturous descriptions of the Atlanta Steam Dye Works, which, he said, "appear in the papers of that city."

The South was suffering from the evils of the reconstruction period following the Civil War. Federal troops were still stationed in Savannah, causing much ill-feeling among the citizens, but almost nothing of all this appears in Joel's lively paragraphs, some of which were like these:

The colored people of Macon celebrated the birthday of Lincoln again on Wednesday. This is the third time since last October.

The Atlanta man who hilariously tempted his mother-in-law to hold a firecracker while he called the children, is now temporarily boarding with his uncle.

The editor of the Cuthbert Appeal, having seen a ten-dollar note, has removed the crape from his arm and announced in his paper that money is becoming easier.

In White County recently, Mr. James H. Trooth had a dispute with a neighbor over some corn. Trooth was crushed to earth, but soon rose again and vanquished his assailant, and now the eternal ears of corn are his.

When the United States had a rather dangerous quarrel with Spain in 1873, Joel wrote:

The bare possibility of a war with Spain has caused some of the valiant roosters who recovered from lameness so suddenly after our late war, to hunt up their old canes. Nothing like being in time.

A humorous warfare with another editor, in which the opponents fired the wittiest retorts they could think of, back and forth at one another, day after day, was a favorite sport of a paragrapher like Joel Harris. Once, when affairs of this sort became rather quiet, he wrote a "want ad":

We desire to engage in a newspaper duel with some respectable person. He must be a man of family and a member of the church. References given and required. No objections to going into the country.

An editor named Shropshire was a favorite antagonist, as another paragraph indicates:

> The Hawkinsville Dispatch, in noticing a local Irish potato, says, "It is nearly as large as some editors' heads we wot of." Why can't these editors let Shropshire alone?

The newspapers in Georgia were all pretty good friends, and, for the most part, enjoyed their controversies immensely. Joel's quips were so much more clever than most of the others that they were widely copied. Every day groups of them were reprinted in other papers, under more or less humorous headings: "Harrisania," "Harrisgraphs," "Harris Sparks," "Red-Top Flashes," "Hot Shots from Red Hair-is." The *Macon Enterprise* quoted them under the heading, "Red Hairs." At which another editor muttered, "Somebody is going to see trouble yet about Harris's head."

But not so. The victim didn't seem to mind, and the nicknames for him, most of them alluding to that hair, were numberless. "Red-Top," "Pink-Top," "Torchlight," "Sorrel-Top," "Vermilion Pate," "Molasses-haired humorist," "Our friend of the ensanguined foretop," "That little crimson pink of the Savannah News," "Burning bush of Georgia journalism," "One of the most valuable contributors to the Southern waste-basket"—these were just a few.

When that curious phenomenon, the Northern Lights, appeared in the sky for two or three nights, an editor announced that he had ascertained that it was not the Aurora Borealis at all, but Pink-Top Harris sailing around over Georgia in a balloon. At another time, Joel admitted having been annoyed, while on a visit to the country, by chigres, those microscopic crimson insects which attack one in the Southern outdoors, and which in Georgia at that time were called "red bugs." Whereupon another joker wrote:

> The impression that Harris of the Savannah News was annoyed by red bugs while at Tallulah is all a mistake. The red bugs saw him coming, thought he was their big brother just got home, and went for him with fraternal embraces.

One editor, describing him, said, "His head is encircled by a halo of redolent glory." But the *Macon Telegraph,* going at the job more satirically, wrote, "J. Chandler Harris, of the Savannah News, stands six feet, five in his stocking feet. He is a brunette of the most perfect type, with coal black hair flowing down his neck in beautiful ringlets."

Once more a serious editor protested that whenever some journalist got the worst of a duel of wits with Harris, "he always falls back on that old, stale, weather-beaten and worn-out repartee, 'red head.' J. C. has one consolation; if his hair *is* red, it is a durned sight more than their articles are."

But very often the other editors paid real tribute to his genius. One called him "the bright, sparkling, vivacious, inimitable Harris. There is no failing in his spirit of wit and humor, playful raillery and pungent sarcasm. As a terse and incisive paragraphist, he is unequaled in the South." "The wit of the press"; "A genius of rare and versatile ability," were other tokens of appreciation.

A subject frequently mentioned in his column was a small-town character named Tump Ponder—some say there really was such a person—the owner of a roan mule, whose heels were so dangerous that his harness had to be put on him with a long pole, and, even then, there had to be a new pole every day, because he wrecked the old one.

Joel was now so widely read that he could start discussions and sensations quite in the manner of today. Once he stirred up much interest over the question, "Who was the prettiest girl in Georgia?" He deftly gave the impression that his "editorial album" was full of photographs of the loveliest beauties of the state. When he went to Eatonton on a visit to his mother, another sharp-eared editor heard of it, and set afloat the story that the brilliant paragrapher of the *Savannah News* had started on a statewide, personal search for that P. G. in G.

But when, shortly after this, he was asked by the press association to respond to the toast, "The Ladies," at the annual banquet, it all turned out just as they might have expected. He at first said no, that he couldn't think of it! Then he began to toy with the idea that he might try the stunt, after all. But as the hour approached, he saw that it was impossible. He went to the dinner, but when the after-dinner oratory came on, it was suddenly discovered that his chair was vacant.

"And this is the man who says so much about the 'P. G. in G!'" jeered a fellow writer. "Fie, Brother Harris! We never in our days heard of a more diabolical case of ignominious desertion."

In his column Joel claimed to be the agent for a newly patented invention, the "chicken torpedo," which would blow up any prowler who tried to steal fowls from a henhouse at night. This brought forth many humorous fake stories, one of them supposed to come from a Baptist minister, who told of rushing to his chicken house after a night explosion and finding many chickens dead and maimed. Grasping the two severed legs of one fowl was a big, black hand, supposedly that of the colored larcenist who was trying to get away with the chickens.

This joke gave birth to a number of new, fanciful titles for Joel—"Colonel J. Craw Harris, President and Treasurer of the Georgia Chicken Torpedo Company"; "Traveling Agent, J. Codrington Harris"; "J. Charlemagne Harris, the inventor" and others.

But the jester also wrote a serious editorial or a literary article at frequent intervals, something whose fineness of conception and crisp beauty of style impressed those who read it. He wrote poems, too, for the paper—always anonymous—both grave and gay, and some of real merit. But the printers said they could always tell when he was writing one of his funny things, for they could hear him laughing in his little den.

One day a prominent citizen of Savannah came to him with a clergyman from Florida, saying, "Mr. Harris, here is a gentleman whom I think you ought to know, and who is very anxious to meet you. He has a communication of unusual importance to make."

The gentleman then went away, and left Joel with the preacher, who proved to be a dry and long-winded talker. After many preliminaries, he finally reached the subject which was nearest his heart.

"The earth is not round, as scientists have always believed," he declared solemnly, "but is shaped like an egg."

Joel, who had been considerably bored, sat up with new interest. He saw that the visitor was what was called in those days a "crank."

"Instead of revolving around the sun," the reverend

gentleman continued, "the earth is the center around which the sun and the whole solar system revolve. The seasons, the periods of heat and cold, are caused by the endosmose and exosmose processes. As you, not being a scientist, may not be familiar with such words as endosmosis, I will explain."

He explained, at great and tiresome length. On and on he maundered, and presently he opened up a package which he carried. Joel saw to his horror that it was a manuscript. There looked to be a ream of it.

"I have written a poem on the subject," said the minister. "I will read portions of it to you."

He cleared his throat and began. Instead of "portions," the unfortunate listener had the impression that he read nearly all of it. It seemed to Joel that the torture would never end, but he was too polite to ask for mercy.

"Now, I have decided," said the gentleman, when he had concluded his reading, "that you are the person to aid me in making known this revolutionary truth to the world. I shall leave the manuscript with you. Study it all at your leisure, publish it in your paper, add your own comments upon it, and it will make us both famous."

He went away, leaving the young scribe flabbergasted. Naturally, the first thing that popped into Joel's head was a satirical comment upon the subject, instead of the grave discussion which the theorist expected. It was a golden opportunity for a youthful humorous paragrapher, but "I ought to have known better," he sighed regretfully in later life.

The irate author called at the *News* office for his manuscript, went up to Chicago or thereabouts, and, for years afterward, took pleasure in launching in the newspapers all sorts of fake stories about Joel, by way of revenge. According to him, "Mr. Harris is a native of Africa, having been born of missionary parents at Joel, on the northeast coast. . . . His hair is snowy white, as the result of a strangely romantic career." He never failed to send his victim a marked copy of the newspaper in which these skits appeared.

Jim Harrison felt Joel's absence from the *Monroe Advertiser* so severely that he went to Savannah to make Joel an offer to return to Forsyth. But naturally, he could not match the salary or the opportunity that Joel had on the *News,* and so nothing came of the proposition.

But Joel, as usual, remembered his former employer with enormous gratitude. He wrote of Jim to Mrs. Starke that "He treated me throughout with a kindness and consideration which I am not sure I deserved."

He also remembered gratefully others at Forsyth—"the friends whom I knew and loved there . . . who were so gentle, so kind and so good, who were always ready to overlook my shortcomings and to forgive my awkward blunders. . . . I know in my soul that I will never again find such friends."

It was always so with Joel. All through life he was convinced that people everywhere had been and were kinder to him than he deserved. He once remarked that he owed everything to the people at Eatonton, who had been so good to him and his mother when he was a child. But he didn't quite mean that. Later, he was to feel just as grateful to Mr. Turner and his family, and then to the people at Macon—and then Forsyth—and so on.

It was natural, too, that one of his temperament should write gloomily to Mrs. Starke soon after he reached

Savannah, "I don't expect to make any friends here—for the simple reason that I shall not try."

But he did, of course. He was soon on very happy terms with all the *News* staff, and he made other acquaintances at the Florida House, a sort of family hotel or boarding house which was his home throughout his stay in Savannah. After he had been there a few months and some of his shyness had worn off, his appearance at the table was welcomed, for the conversation immediately became livelier and wittier.

One of his close friends at the boarding house was Louis Weber, a young pharmacist and clerk in one of the city's drug stores. Their rooms on the fourth floor were next to each other. Both had to work until late at night, Joel a little later than Weber, who would always sit up until his friend came. Then they would discuss politics or literature or read aloud to each other from some new book and criticize it. Or, on rare occasions, when they were feeling frolicsome, they might indulge in a bit of singing or skylarking.

On Sundays, the most thrilling recreation was a stroll on Bull Street, the city's main residence boulevard. They had a funny little tradition in Savannah. It was an unwritten rule that the sidewalk on the west side of Bull Street was reserved as a promenade for the aristocracy; the east side was for the lower classes. Joel and Louis dressed up in their best clothes and walked on both sides.

CHAPTER SEVENTEEN

Romance

AMONG the boarders at the Florida House were a
middle-aged couple, Captain Pierre La Rose and
his wife, Mrs. Esther Dupont La Rose. They
were French Canadians by birth, and their charming per-
sonalities and piquant pronunciation made them quite
popular. Captain La Rose was the operator of a steamboat,
the *Lizzie Baker,* which ran from Savannah down the
coast and up the St. John's River to Palatka. He also owned
some large farms in the Province of Quebec. They had three
children, but for a long time Joel saw only two of them.

"Our oldest daughter, Esther—she is nearly sixteen—
is at school in St. Hyacinthe in Quebec," Mrs. La Rose told
him.

"Is she a native of Canada, too?" asked Joel.

"No sir," replied the Captain, "she was born when we
were living in Lansingburg, near Troy, New York. That
was in 1854. I was running two boats, the *John Tracy* and
the *Edmund Lewis,* on the Hudson River then.

"After the Civil War began, and the Federals got possession of the mouth of the James River, I took the *John Tracy*
down to Washington and carried mail and supplies be-

tween there and the army. I would sail from Washington down to Newport News, or whatever port near by the Union army was using. Going back, there would usually be a load of Confederate prisoners and wounded soldiers of both armies, poor fellows, on their way north to prisons and hospitals. In summer they lay on the open deck; sometimes it was covered with them. Picture it to yourself, Mr. Harris. The sun may be very hot in Virginia, and the suffering of those sick and wounded men tore at my heart. One day some Southern wounded prisoners in their agony begged to be thrown overboard."

The Captain's voice rose in his excitement.

"I protested to the army officer in charge of them. 'It is inhuman!' I cried. 'You should provide shelter for them or not send them north in such hot weather.'"

"Papa!" admonished Mrs. La Rose. "You are talking too loud."

"He was angry," said the Captain, lowering his voice with terrific effort. "He bade me attend to my own affairs. I saw by his look at me that he meant me no good. And sure enough, he reported to the War Department that I was a rebel sympathizer. Soldiers came to my boat and arrested me, and I was thrown into the old Capitol Prison."

The Captain's arms fell into his lap in tragic despair.

"Do you know Washington, Mr. Harris? No? Then you do not know that old brick building they called the Capitol Prison. A terrible place! The filth! The rats! The bugs! I cannot tell you about it. . . .

"When my wife, who was up at Lansingburg, heard of my troubles, she hurried down to Washington. Someone said to her, 'When you want justice in Washington, when you need kindness and understanding, do not go to any minor official. Go right to President Lincoln.' And so she did.

"Ah, there was a great man, Mr. Harris! What a pity he was not allowed to live! How much better off the South would be now! Of course, he received my Esther. He received anyone who went to him in trouble. She told him that I acted only from humanity. 'We are French Canadians, Mr. President,'' she said. 'We care little for your politics down here. But my husband was in your government's service, and whatever work he goes into, he is loyal to it. He is not two-faced. If you had been in his place, Mr. President,' she said, leaning over and looking into those sad eyes, 'I know that you would have done just as he did.'

"Well, you can guess what Mr. Lincoln did. He issued the order for my release at once, and I went back to my boat. A little later I sold the *John Tracy* and the *Edmund Lewis*. After the war I came down here and bought the *Lizzie Baker* and started operating it. I have a captain on the boat, but I cannot resist making most of the trips with it. The water and I, we belong to each other."

For nearly two years Joel did not see the older daughter. In late spring at just about the time for her school term to close, Mrs. La Rose and the two younger children would join her in Canada, and they would spend the summer on one of their farms.

But in the second spring, Essie came down to Savannah at the close of her school, and one glimpse of her changed the whole aspect of life for Joel. She was small and dainty, with sparkling, dark eyes and brown hair in ringlets. She played the piano and sang prettily. She had the most delicious little touch of a French Canadian accent that one ever heard.

Joel was completely captivated. He began shyly to linger after meals to talk to her, and finally became bold enough to tease and joke with her. But there were times when he was perfectly convinced that she could never take him seriously. He was very gloomy over the prospect. He would take Louis Weber out to a cemetery—as being the place most suitable to his state of mind—and there sitting on an old flat gravestone, he would pour out his feelings, telling of his love and the complete hopelessness of it.

"She has many beaux, Louis," he would wail. "They just swarm around her. What chance has a homely, stammering, redheaded country lout with those stylish fellows?"

Louis listened and consoled him. He was too good a friend to let it be seen that the moonstruck lover was rather boring.

Liking Joel as they did, and knowing of his excellent position and prospects, Essie's parents made no objection to his going out with her. Among her many admirers they did not think he could be a very serious contender. His greatest difficulty was with the young lady herself. She was something of a coquette, and her sudden changes of attitude toward him, her kindness toward other admirers, nearly drove him wild at times.

A style of dress called "Dolly Varden"—after the heroine of Dickens's novel, *Barnaby Rudge*—was a great fad at that time, and Essie was particularly attractive in it. Joel wrote an anonymous poem for the *News*, which had her for its subject, though none of the readers of the paper knew it, and probably thought the writer was just describing a "type":

An Idyl of the Period

Oh, surely you have met her
At the Park or on the street—
She wears her hair in jaunty curls
And dresses deuced neat.

Her Grecian bend's a bouncer,
And her hat's the merest scrap
Of silk and straw and ribbon—but
She doesn't "care a snap."

She sports a Dolly Varden
Of yellow, red and green,
And skips along in bronze bootees,
The neatest ever seen.

When she thrids the crowded pavement,
You can hear her flounces flap,
As she boldly swings her parachute,
But she doesn't "care a snap."

The boys call her "a stunner,"
And many a love-lorn chap
Tips his beaver as she passes—but,
She doesn't "care a snap."

And her epitaph will be,
When Death's cold hand shall rap
Upon her varnished chamber door:
"She never cared a snap."

The "Grecian bend," a slight stoop forward, affected by ladies when they walked, was another fad of the day.

Essie's shrewd mind saw the worthy soul beneath the awkward exterior of the young fellow boarder. If there was ever any doubt as to his intellect, his writings for the paper were enough to remove that. Within a few weeks Joel thought he had reason to believe that he had found a place in her heart. But then she would smile at some other fellow or go out walking with him, and Joel would take Louis out to the cemetery and sit on a tombstone and tell him another tale of woe.

Now he heard to his consternation that in June Mrs. La Rose and the three children would go to Canada as usual to spend the summer. He began—hesitatingly, of course—to sound Essie to see whether she would write to him while she was away. Sometimes she seemed to say yes, and at other times no. He didn't know what to think. On the morning of her departure he was at home, but so overcome by—he knew not what—that he could not say farewell to her. He shut himself up in his room, but, listening at the door, had the agony of hearing her exchange goodbys with Louis—Louis, the rascal, as cool as a cucumber meanwhile—and adding, "Tell Mr. Harris good-by for me, if he cares to hear of me."

"If he cares!" Joel buried his head under his pillow and kicked himself for being so inept.

On the day after her departure, he began writing a journal to be sent to her, recording some of his doings but more of his thoughts. In a day or two he decided that she couldn't possibly be interested in such junk, so he wrote her a letter instead. Later on, he sent her the journal, too.

It was written with the best literary skill that he possessed, and it declared his love as fervently as his letters had done. But Essie didn't write as often as he thought she should, he complained of it, and she ceased to write at all.

When she returned in the autumn, more beautiful than ever, there were rumors that she had a suitor in Canada. The sight of her, the sound of her voice made him ready to forget and forgive everything. He began eagerly seeking a few words with her after meals each day. Then she consented to give him one evening a week. She was so understanding, so sympathetic, so in tune with his humorous view of life that in her company he forgot his self-consciousness and was perfectly at ease.

It soon became evident that she loved him, and not many weeks had passed before he had her answer, "Yes—if Papa consents."

There was the rub. In those days, especially in the case of a girl as young as Essie, and one brought up as she had been, you had to ask Papa, too. Fancy Joel's terror at such an ordeal! For days he strove to nerve himself to it. Then he began trying to catch Captain La Rose alone, but the wily shipmaster had guessed what was up, and, reluctant to give up his daughter, deftly avoided him.

Finally the time came when the question could not be deferred any longer. Trailing the Captain stealthily from the dinner table through the long hall of the Florida House, Joel caught him alone near the front door. Red as a lobster and stuttering furiously, he hurled his request at Essie's father like a grenade:

"C-c-c-captain, I w-want to m-m-marry your d-d-daughter."

The Captain had been expecting something of the sort, but that didn't make the news any easier when it came. In his excitement, he became more French than usual.

"Eempossible!" he exclaimed, throwing up his hands. "She ees too yong!"

"B-b-but—"

"She knows nothing of housekeeping."

"S-she c-can learn."

"You are both too yong to take care of yourselves."

"I've t-taken c-care of myself for ten years," Joel reminded him. "I g-guess I can take care of her."

"But she is a Catholic and you are a Protestant."

"I d-don't belong to any church," declared Joel. "D-does it make any difference, anyhow?"

"Does it—" The Captain, waving his arms, lost his English and burst into French. Finally, the storm having passed, he regained control of himself. He faced the inevitable, and said, "Well, if she wants to marry you, I leave it with her."

Privately, however, he tried to stave off the event, in the hope that the lovers might change their minds. "You should not be in a hurry," he said to Essie. "I will give you a trip to Europe—Paris, Switzerland, Rome. . . ."

"That would be very nice, Papa," said Essie, "but I think I would rather stay at home and marry Joel."

The Captain's hands fell into his lap in tragic despair.

That had been an eventful summer for young Harris. He had risen to the top of the editorial staff so rapidly that Colonel Thompson, when he went away on his vacation, left him in charge, and other editors, as well as readers, said they could see no letdown in the quality of the paper.

In 1872 a wing of the Republican Party nominated

"Eempossible!" he exclaimed. "She ees too yong!"

Horace Greeley, the New York editor, for President. Greeley had very quickly forgiven the South for its secession, and was opposed to the Republican leaders who were bent upon punishing the former Confederates. Just after this, Colonel Thompson went on his vacation, leaving Joel at the helm. One day a surprising telegram was delivered at the *News* office.

"What do you think of this?" said the staff man who opened it. "The Democrats have nominated Greeley, too."

"I was expecting it," said Joel slowly, "but I'll not support a Republican. He fought us too hard during the war."

So as the days went on, the *News* said nothing about Greeley or the campaign. It was unprecedented. Many people of the South were against Greeley, too, but the politicians in the state insisted that the *News* ought to back the party nominee—or back somebody, at least. Joel, who didn't like politicians anyhow, calmly went on writing editorials on other subjects. The country editors were at a loss, for many of them took their tone from the *News* and followed its ideas.

"Look here, Joe," said Colonel Estill, the owner of the paper, "the party leaders and the editors are getting all stirred up because we don't take a stand. Seems to me you ought to do something."

"Colonel," said Joel, calmly leaning back in his chair, "I'm against this Greeley nomination, and I'm not going to support it. Colonel Thompson left me in command, and as long as I'm in this chair, I will say nothing for Greeley. When the chief comes back, he may do as he likes. If you want to replace me—"

"Oh no! No!" protested Colonel Estill, and went away,

marveling at the stubbornness of a young man who ordi-
narily seemed so meek and mild. Colonel Thompson returned in a few days, and the very next morning the *News*
took its stand for Greeley. There was no friction over the
incident, and Joel didn't greatly care about the paper's
attitude. He had been true to his own beliefs, and that was
all that mattered.

In the following spring, on April 21, 1873, just as the
magnolia and jasmine and azalea and japonica and
bougainvillaea were in a riot of bloom, Joel and Essie were
quietly married in the parlor of the Florida House, with
only Louis and a select few of the boarders as guest wit-
nesses. Papa La Rose gave the bridegroom a big, hand-
somely chased silver watch, of a type that was popular
then, and he carried it for the rest of his life.

When the Georgia editors heard of the event, there came
a flood of sincere congratulations and not a little joking.

"Marriage has not dulled Harris's wit," wrote one con-
temporary. "He has launched out lately in a brighter and
saucier style than ever." His friend, Henry W. Grady of
the *Atlanta Herald,* thought another twelve months would
tame him down, and jested about his buying ormolu
clocks—a favorite wedding gift of those days—for other
brides through the coming years.

Henry Grady was destined to play a large part in Joel's
life. They had met a few years before, when both were boy
editors, Joel at Forsyth, and Henry, only eighteen, was
actually editing the leading paper in Rome, Georgia. They
became acquainted through their editorial teasing of each
other, wrote a few letters back and forth, and finally Joel,
taking a short vacation, went by Rome, picked up Grady,

and they journeyed to Chattanooga and Lookout Mountain on a jovial sightseeing trip. In print Joel usually referred to his friend as Col. H. Whiffletree Grady.

Two children were born to Joel and Esther in the next two years, sons who were named Julian and Lucien. Father La Rose, thinking his son-in-law should be at the head of his own establishment, wanted to buy a small-town newspaper for him.

"I've looked into the matter," he said. "There are papers in La Grange and Monroe that can be bought, and I will gladly buy one of them for you. There you would be your own boss, and you could make a paper that everybody in the state would want."

"No thanks, Father," said Joel. "It's very kind of you, but I'd rather stand on my own feet. I think my best opportunity is on a city newspaper, anyhow."

About this time he even dallied a little with the idea of going to New York. It is likely that he could have made a success there, but he would never have been happy there. New York was too big, too far from and too unlike Georgia.

And then came the catastrophe which swept him out of Savannah involuntarily. In 1875 yellow fever leaped over from the West Indies to Key West, Florida, and a few cases even appeared in New York City. No one knew how to prevent the spread of the disease then, for this was more than twenty-five years before Dr. Walter Reed and his associates discovered that the yellow-fever germ is carried by a certain type of mosquito.

In the summer of 1876 the dreaded disease appeared again on the Gulf Coast and crept rapidly northward. The first case appeared in Savannah on August 21st. It spread with terrifying rapidity, and within a few days people were dying of it. Between that time and the end of the epidemic late in November, 1,600 white persons died of the plague in Savannah. It was not nearly so fatal to the colored people. In fact, many of them seemed immune to it.

As soon as the epidemic took hold on a Southern city in those days, some of the citizens began fleeing northward. There were many who could not afford to leave, and there were others who grimly stuck by their work and took their chance.

Joel might have been one of these had it not been for his concern for his family. As the situation grew more terrifying, he could not endure the thought of exposing Essie and the children to it for another day. So they packed their belongings, and on a crowded train they hurried through a frightened countryside—at many stations there were guards to prevent passengers from Savannah from getting off—to Atlanta, which was not invaded by the disease.

At Atlanta they settled down—though they did not realize it at the time—to spend the rest of their lives. It was a wrench to leave Savannah and the *News,* which had grown very dear to them. Colonel Thompson, after the scourge was over, begged Harris to come back to the paper, but Joel was afraid to expose his family to the menace of yellow fever, and furthermore, the epidemic had been so disastrous to business in Savannah that the *News* was not able to offer him his old salary. Atlanta was a rapidly growing city, and the time soon came when Joel was glad that he had made the change.

Savannah was long jealous of the upstart young city up the country, which had by smart politics taken the State capitol away from Milledgeville and had risen from its wartime ashes to pass Savannah in population and become one of the leading cities of the South.

Joel, with his love of a joke, got some fun out of this whenever he could. Twenty years after he left Savannah, he went back there on a business trip. He arrived in the morning and went to a restaurant for breakfast. He was seated at a table with three elderly men, one of whom, sitting beside him, he recognized as a friend of other days. The old gentleman, however, did not recognize his friend Harris, who had grown much heavier and changed from youth to middle age.

Joel began to seethe inwardly with fun at once. While waiting to be served, he turned with an innocent face to the old acquaintance beside him and asked blandly, "What town is this, sir?"

The three men stared in amazement. The old gentleman shuffled his feet perplexedly and finally said, "I didn't catch your remark, sir."

"I asked the name of the town," said Joel, his round chubby face still beaming with innocence. "I think it's a very pretty place."

"It is Savannah, sir! Savannah!" said the old gentleman in a deep and awful voice.

One of the other men leaned an elbow on the table and, fixing the stranger with his eyes, said, "And what part of the country may you be from, sir?"

"Atlanta," replied Joel. The effect was electric. The horrified indignation on the three other faces was appalling. The old gentleman next to Joel beckoned to the waiter.

"George," he said, "take my breakfast to another table."

"Why, Mr. ——!" exclaimed Joel, calling him by name. "You wouldn't have treated me this way twenty years ago."

The old man glared in amazement. "Who are you?" he asked, finding his voice at last.

"Joe Harris," was the meek reply.

The rage upon the old man's brow melted into plain astonishment and then into pleasure. He burst into a roar of laughter. He pounded Joel's back, he shook his hand again and again; he introduced him to the two other men, to whom, by that time, the name of Joel Chandler Harris was as well known as that of the President. He thought it the best joke of the year.

"He even paid for my breakfast," chuckled Joel, in telling of the incident.

CHAPTER EIGHTEEN

The Birth of Uncle Remus

W HEN the Harrises reached Atlanta, they went to the Kimball House, then the leading hotel, where the husband and father solemnly registered:

> J. C. Harris, one wife, two bow-legged children and a bilious nurse.

Of course the joke was being told all over town in a few days.

The hotel was crowded with refugees from the yellow-fever cities. The optimism and jesting of the Savannah editor had such a good effect upon the gloom of these other folk that when Joel went to the desk to pay his bill upon leaving, the manager said, "Mr. Harris, you don't owe us a cent. You've been such a good influence here that we're indebted to you *at least three dollars' worth!*"

But we do not hear that this magnificent sum was ever paid to the genial guest.

Jim Harrison, his old employer at Forsyth, was now

living at Decatur, only a few miles out of Atlanta. He and his wife extended a typical, old-time Southern invitation, the sort which was accepted as readily as it was given.

"Bring your family out and visit with us until you get your bearings," they said, and thither the Harrises went.

Jim, a good businessman, had left Forsyth and risen rapidly. Mr. James P. Harrison was now president of a printing and publishing company which issued several papers, among them *The Granger,* an organ of a farmers' political movement of the period.

"Come around and make yourself at home in the office, Joe," he invited. "I'll have a desk rigged up for you. If you care to write anything for *The Granger* or our religious or children's papers, we will be mighty proud of it and glad to pay you for it."

And thus Joel picked up a few dollars. He also wrote some bits for the Atlanta newspapers and did some correspondence for the *Savannah News.*

Soon after arriving, he met his friend, Henry Grady, on the street in Atlanta. Henry was accompanied by an older man.

"Joel," he said, "let me introduce one of our Georgia senators, Mr. Ben H. Hill."

Joel blushed, for he had often cracked jokes in his column at Mr. Hill's expense. Now he saw the Senator drawing an old leather wallet from his pocket. He took a clipping from it.

"Young man," he said, "did you write that?"

Joel looked at it and blushed more redly than ever—one of those blushes, as they used to say, when you couldn't tell where his face ended and his hair began. The paragraph was a recent one, which treated in a good-natured manner an unfortunate incident in which Mr. Hill had been involved.

"Y-yes sir, I did," admitted Joel.

"I own a block of stock in the Kimball House, Mr. Harris," said the Senator. "You may go there, register, and tell the clerk to charge your board to B. H. Hill as long as you want to stay."

All of which showed that Senator Hill had a broad and generous mind and a sense of humor.

"And how are things with you?" asked Joel of Henry Grady, after more talk.

"Not very good at present," was the reply. *"The Herald* has collapsed, and I am out of a job. But Captain Evan P. Howell is about to buy a controlling interest in the *Constitution*. That will mean some changes, and I am hoping to find a place there. Maybe there will be something there for you, too, Joe."

He had already said to Howell, "Do you know that the most brilliant paragrapher in Georgia is here in the city and at liberty?" The captain who knew something of Joel's work, thereupon sought him out and said, "You are not going back to Savannah, Mr. Harris. You are going to stay right here and join the *Constitution's* staff."

Sure enough, when Howell completed his deal for the *Constitution,* he engaged Henry Grady for the staff. Within two years Grady was made editor in chief, and to the day of his death his name was inseparable from that of the *Constitution*.

"I want you to write a column for us, Mr. Harris," said Captain Howell, "but we're a young organization here, and I can offer you only twenty-five dollars a week. I hope I can make it more before long."

Joel talked it over with Essie. "It's a lot less than I've been getting," he said, "and I hate to leave Savannah. But on the other hand, I don't want to be running from the yellow fever every little while, and maybe having it catch up with us some time. I think I'd better stay here."

When the news of his engagement spread, congratulations poured in upon the *Constitution* from all parts of the South. Immediately, he began chaffing his old town with such bits as "Savannah has had its regular triweekly robbery."

To help the family finances, he also worked for a while at night as telegraph editor, which added five dollars a week more to his income. As soon as he had obtained his job, Joel found a house in the city, the rent for which was not too high; then he and Essie shopped for some cheap furniture and set up housekeeping. Essie knew nothing about the management of a home, for they had lived in a hotel during their stay in Savannah. But with the assistance of a colored maid and of Grandmother Harris, who now came up from Eatonton to live with them, she learned rapidly. She proved to have a good head for business, so the family finances were well managed.

And Grandmother not only gave advice, but also told the two little boys thrilling stories of earlier days, how she once rode horseback with her parents to Tennessee on a visit, passing through the Cherokee Indian country; and how, when she was living alone at Eatonton, she kept a hatchet in her bedroom for protection, and one night threw it at a prowler whom she heard in the garden.

The Howells were their near neighbors, and they quickly became such close friends that the third son, who was born soon after they settled in Atlanta, was christened Evan

Howell. But the little one died when he was only a year and a half old. A fourth son, Evelyn, was born in 1878.

When Joel went to the *Constitution,* he was twenty-eight years old. Howell, the owner, was in his late thirties, and Henry Grady was twenty-six. They were all vivacious in temperament, and had a lot of fun together. Forenoons, when they met to begin the day's work, they would first assemble, perhaps in Joel's room. Lounging about, usually with one sitting on a corner of the desk, they would enjoy a "kidding" session—teasing, tossing jokes, and repartee at one another, and laughing uproariously. Refreshed by several minutes of this, they would then have the real editorial conference on the day's policy and go to their desks.

Under Grady and Harris the *Constitution* became the most influential journal in the South. They both labored to bring immigration and industry down there from the Northern states, and it was Joel's particular care to heal the wounds caused by the Civil War and bring about a better understanding between the Yankees and the Rebs. President Theodore Roosevelt once said of him that "one of his greatest services is that he has written what exalts the South in the mind of every man who reads it, and yet which has not a flavor of bitterness toward any other part of the Union."

After he had been in Atlanta a little more than two years, Joel found opportunity to write a column called "The Lounger" in the *Sunday Gazette.* It touched in a rambling way upon nature, literature, the drama, and other topics. It was not signed, but another editor said, "There is only one man in Georgia who could have written it—Joel Chandler Harris." This writer saw in it a likeness to the essays of Charles Lamb, and also a dramatic crispness like that of Bret Harte.

But in the meantime its writer had found the vein of ore which soon made him famous. A man named Sam Small had been conducting in the *Constitution* a column of sketches and jokes in which a Negro character, "Uncle Si," appeared. Small withdrew from the paper soon after Captain Howell took it over.

"Joe," said the proprietor, "can't you carry on this Uncle Si series of Sam's? It has quite an audience."

Joel did not feel enthusiastic. "I don't think I can continue another man's idea," said he. "I don't seem to know Uncle Si. But I'll do something similar, perhaps with a character of my own." The truth of the matter was that he didn't care for Small's delineation of the Negro.

His first contributions in this line were dialect poems, songs which he had heard from the plantation Negroes, and to which he made certain additions of his own. The first one that appeared was a revival song which began:

Oh, whar shill we go w'en de great day comes,
Wid de blowin' er de trunpits en de bangin' er de **drums?**
How many po' sinners 'll be kotched out late
En fine no latch ter de golden gate?
No use fer ter wait twel ter-morrer!
De sun must n't set on yo' sorrer,
Sin 's ez sharp ez a bamboo-brier—
Oh, Lord! fetch de mo'ners up higher!

This was copied all over the country and much enjoyed. It was even stolen and its authorship credited to a man in a small town in New York.

Other songs followed, and then an old Negro character appeared. As he began to take form in the author's mind, the name of the old gardener in Forsyth, "Uncle Remus," popped into his head—and so a noted figure in literature was born.

At first Uncle Remus was represented as an elderly man, a former slave, who lived in Atlanta, who dropped in at the *Constitution* office occasionally, or talked with his friends on the street, telling of his experiences and voicing his philosophy. The sketches were all humorous.

But while he was writing these, Joel read in *Lippincott's Magazine* an article on the folklore of the Southern Negroes. It mentioned their animal stories and gave rough outlines of a few of them, but there was no attempt made to tell them in dialect.

Lacking something else to write on one occasion, Joel wrote down one of the stories which he had heard from Uncle George or Uncle Bob Capers, or perhaps from both of them, for he had heard some of these stories time and again. This was in 1879. It was the tale of how Br'er Fox tried to cajole Br'er Rabbit by saying that they ought to be better friends, and even accepted an invitation to dine at Br'er Rabbit's house, but was so obviously intending to make a meal of his host or some of the family that Br'er Rabbit had to outwit him—as usual.

"I hadn't any idea that the things would make much of a hit," he told his wife. "But it seems to be well liked"— which was a characteristic understatement.

He wrote another one, and then another one. Always the stories were told by Uncle Remus—who lived alone in his cabin on the old plantation—to a little boy, the son of the proprietor. There was a close friendship between the little chap and the old man who loved him dearly, and saw in him resemblance to "Ol' Miss," the boy's grandmother.

Some people, when they learned that Joel had heard the stories in boyhood, thought that he himself had been the original of the little boy, some thought that his son Julian had sat for the picture, but neither surmise was right. In a letter to his old playmate, Joe Syd Turner, written several years later, the author said, "Did it never occur to you that *you* might be the little boy of 'Uncle Remus'? I suppose you have forgotten the comical tricks you played on old George Terrell, and the way you wheedled him out of a part of his ginger cakes and cider. . . . Those were the wonderfullest days we shall ever see!"

But now he found that the stories were creating a stir in the land. Newspapers, both North and South, were copying them. The *New York Evening Post* was particularly interested in them. It copied so many and made so much comment upon them that the author in a grateful letter to the editors said, "I feel that if the *Evening Post* had not taken up Uncle Remus, his legends would have attracted little or no attention."

But this was just an example of Joel Harris's modesty. Another is seen in his amazement when a representative of a big New York publishing house came all the way down to Atlanta and suggested that the Uncle Remus stories be put into a book. The author was almost incredulous.

"But he seemed to be in earnest," said Joel, in telling of the creation of the book. "And so we picked out of the files of the *Constitution* enough matter for a little volume, and it was printed. To my surprise, it was successful."

When the publishers chose Frederick S. Church, a

popular illustrator of the day, to draw the pictures for the book, Joel thought that if it had any sale at all, it would be because of Church's drawings. He wrote to the artist, congratulating himself on the selection, and saying, "I was afraid you were too busy to give your attention to such trifles."

When the book, *Uncle Remus, His Songs and Sayings,* was published in 1880, he was still more astonished at the notice which it attracted, especially from learned men all over the world. Even while the stories were being printed in the *Constitution,* a man who was an authority on the folklore of the Indians along the Amazon River, wrote to him, telling of many of the South American Indian legends which were almost identical with those of our Southern plantations.

In these stories, the tortoise was most often the hero, and his exploits were very closely like those of Br'er Tarrypin; as when he won a ten-mile race from the deer, for example, by precisely the same trick which Br'er Tarrypin worked on Br'er Rabbit. This was done by stationing one of his family—they all looked so much alike that no one could tell them apart—at the starting point, and at every mile post along the course, so that it would seem that he was keeping up with the deer. The old tortoise himself was hidden in the grass near the finish, and crawled out just in time to give the appearance of winning the race.

Joel remarked later that when he began writing these stories, "I did not know much about folklore, and I didn't think that anybody else did." But he soon had plenty of evidence to the contrary.

A learned philologist said that variants of the story of Br'er Fox and the Tar Baby which he made to catch Br'er

Rabbit had been found among the Indians of both North and South America and of the West Indies, in various parts of Africa, from the Cape of Good Hope up past the Congo to the Niger region, and in India. An army officer wrote that he had heard stories like "Uncle Remus's" among the Moros in the Philippines. In fact, it seemed that those simple folk legends might be among the oldest stories in the world.

From nearer home, the author received letters which warmed his heart. Alexander H. Stephens, the Georgia statesman who had been Vice President of the Confederate States, wrote to him, "My father had an old family servant whose name was Ben. . . . Often have I sat up late at nights in his house and heard nearly every one of those stories about Br'er Rabbit, Br'er Fox, and Br'er Terrapin, as you have reproduced them. In reading them, I have been living my young life over again."

Mr. Stephens had been clipping the stories and pasting them in a scrapbook from the time when they first began appearing in the *Constitution*.

A Southern author told of visiting a Georgia plantation and finding a young lady, a daughter of the family, seated in the midst of a group of little colored children, reading aloud the "Uncle Remus" stories "to the most delighted audience you ever saw. . . ." It seemed an odd and whimsical thing to him—"A Southern girl reading to little Negroes stories which had come down from the dead fathers of their race."

CHAPTER NINETEEN

Rising Fame

OVER and over again, as praise for his genius came flooding in on him, the dazed creator of "Uncle Remus" protested, "I'm not an author, I'm just a journalist who writes down what he hears." He would mention the articles in *Lippincott's Magazine* which gave him the idea of writing the "Uncle Remus" stories, and say:

"This was the accidental beginning of a career that has been accidental throughout. It was an accident that I went to the *Countryman,* an accident that I wrote Uncle Remus, and an accident that the stories put forth under that name struck the popular fancy."

But others knew better. They knew that he was not a mere phonograph nor an accident. They knew that he could not remember all those stories, word for word, but must re-tell them, re-create much of the humor and tricks of dialect of the old-time Negro, and fill in the forgotten nooks where necessary. They knew that to do this, to create the character of "Uncle Remus," and the byplay between him and the little boy, required genius.

Mark Twain—who wrote a letter expressing admiration of the stories—told him all this. The overmodest creator of Uncle Remus replied, "Everybody has been kind to the old man, but you have been kindest of all. I am perfectly well aware that my book has no basis of literary art to stand upon; I know it is the matter and not the manner that has attracted public attention and won the consideration of people of taste at the North."

"Mark Twain," whose real name was Clemens, replied in effect that "you may argue *yourself* into that notion, but you are the only convert you will make." And he added:

" 'Uncle Remus' is most deftly drawn and is a lovable and delightful creation; he and the little boy and their relations with each other are bright, fine literature, and worthy to live. . . . But I seem to be proving to the man that made the multiplication table that twice one is two."

Mr. Clemens gave Joel a ghost story which had been told him by an old Negro in his boyhood, with privilege to use it, and suggested that they two appear on the lecture platform together, each giving readings from his own works. He was going to New Orleans soon, and he asked if Mr. Harris wouldn't meet him there and talk it over.

Joel at first took the proposition seriously. There were fine fees to be earned on the lecture platform in those days, and the Harris family needed money. What with three growing boys and a girl baby recently born, the rented house in the city was getting pretty crowded. The fine reception which the critics had given the Uncle Remus book encouraged its author to buy a home of his own.

"There's a place not far from my home, Joe," said Captain Howell. "Rather run down now, but you can fix it up."

Joel went out to look at it, and wanted it at once.

"It's out in what they call West End," he reported enthusiastically to his wife. "It's really in the country—

close to the end of a car line, though. I've always wanted to live in the country. Best place to bring up youngsters, too."

"What sort of place is it?" she asked.

"Five and a quarter acres," he recited glibly. "Six-room house, ground slopes down nicely to the road, beautiful pine woods close by the house, fine spring just across the road."

"What will it cost?"

"Twenty-five hundred dollars, and we can buy it on easy terms."

But when Essie saw it she almost shed tears. "Oh Joel," she cried in disappointment. The house was cheap, common; ugly, built on no particular plan, and tall weeds almost hid it from the road. Its interior had been painted a hideous green, it was in bad repair, and infested by rats.

"And that street car is blocks and blocks away," the young wife wailed, "and you have to ride half an hour on it to get downtown."

"But look! We walk through that lovely woods to reach the car line," her husband urged, "and they say the line's going to be extended some day soon. We can remodel the house—"

"And that will cost more money!"

"And look at the beautiful location—the pine woods— the space for the children to play in. We can have a vegetable garden—and flowers. . . ."

She saw all that very readily. It was only that she had *so* wanted to move into a nice house! But she was not hard to convince. The house was repainted, the rat holes eliminated, the yard cleaned up, and the family moved in. This was in the summer of 1881.

The thought of that mortgage hanging over him was why the new home owner at first considered seriously Mark Twain's proposal that they do public readings together. He went down to New Orleans to meet the great humorist and talk it over. They went one day to the home of another famous writer, George W. Cable, who had invited some children in to meet the creator of the beloved Uncle Remus, and hear the Tar Baby story from his own lips. But when the time came to stand up and read, he was overcome with shyness, as anybody might have known he would be. All one big blush, he gasped in undertones, "I c-can't! I j-just c-can't do it!"

"Come on! It's easy," urged the others. "Just a lot of children . . ."

But there were some ladies there, too, with the children, and there were two noted authors, and— Well, he just couldn't muster up the courage.

"Come! We'll read something from our own stuff, to show you how easy it is," said Mark.

So he read a chapter from *Huckleberry Finn,* and Mr. Cable read something of his own. But even that did not help.

"I can't do it!" still protested the scared author. "You read it for me." And so Mark Twain had to read to the children about Br'er Rabbit and the Tar Baby.

That ended all thought of Joel Harris's appearing on the lecture platform. His unconquerable bashfulness and the frightened stutter which was sure to attack him when he was in the presence of a crowd made such hopes impossible.

His rising fame was not only bringing him an increased income, but also some more uncomfortable moments when he had to listen to praise of himself. Walter Hines Page, later a great publisher and United States Ambassador to Great Britain, but then a young journalist, went down to Atlanta to interview him. At first he found it difficult to believe that the shy, quiet man whom he discovered smoking a cigar in the editorial rooms was the great author.

"A little man just turned thirty-one," so Mr. Page described him, "with red hair, a fiery, half-vicious mustache, a freckled face and freckled hands. His eyes are all that belongs to Mr. Joel C. Harris: all other things, hair, complexion, hands, chin and manner, are the property of Joe Harris."

When the visitor told him how much pleasure Northern people were getting from Uncle Remus, the author blushed and stammered:

"They have been very kind to Uncle Remus."

"It was impossible to believe," wrote Mr. Page, "that the man realized what he had done. I afterward discovered that his most appreciative friends held the same opinion; that Joe Harris does not appreciate Joel Chandler Harris."

Now editors were begging for his work. He contributed more Uncle Remus stories and "plantation ballads" to the *Century, Harper's,* and other noted magazines. His stock of animal stories ran low, and he wrote to friends and acquaintances here and there, asking if they could scrape up any new ones for him. One lady down on the seacoast below Savannah was especially helpful. But as the Negroes along the Georgia and Carolina coast speak a dialect called "Gullah," which is much different from that of the interior, Joel had to translate these into middle Georgia speech.

However, he decided to tell some of them in their original dialect, and to do this he introduced a new character, Daddy Jack, a very old man who was supposed to have been born in Africa. Some evenings, according to the author, Daddy Jack, Tildy the housemaid, and fat, jolly Aunt Tempy all gathered in Uncle Remus's cabin, and their conversation with one another was almost as funny as their stories, for each of the visitors thought of a story to tell now and then.

Joel even went to the Negroes themselves for some new tales. He had found that no Negro, when approached by a stranger, would admit knowing any of this lore. He also had learned, as many another writer has learned, that the best way to induce shy people to tell stories is to "prime the pump" by telling one yourself of the sort you want.

One summer evening he was at a little railroad station in Georgia, waiting to catch a train. About thirty Negroes who were employed on the railroad were around the end of the station, some sitting on the edge of the platform, some on a pile of cross ties near by. All, as usual, were in high good humor, cracking jokes at one another and laughing uproariously.

The solitary white man sat down on the edge of the platform next one of the liveliest talkers of the group. Presently, when someone mentioned "Old Molly Har' "—a joking way of speaking of Br'er Rabbit's wife—Joel began telling the man next him the Tar Baby story. He told it in a low tone, as if too modest to ask for the attention of the whole crowd. But his listener, delighted, would exclaim every minute or so, "Dar now!" or "He's a honey, mon!" or "Git outer de way, gentermens, and gin him room!" and mingling these remarks with loud laughter.

This quickly drew the attention of the other Negroes, and they began to gather round the two to listen. Joel followed the first story with the one about Br'er Rabbit and the mosquitoes, illustrating it with the numerous slaps which Br'er Rabbit made at the tormenting insects when he was calling on Miss Wolf at Br'er Wolf's home down in the swamp.

This brought shouts of laughter from the audience, but there were two or three who could scarcely wait for the end of it, so anxious were they to tell stories of their own. Others followed them, and for two hours the happy author sat there, listening to them. Some of them he had already heard and had put into print. But most of them were new. Some of the men were poor storytellers; others, so Joel declared, were better than Uncle Remus himself.

It was impossible to take notes, for two reasons. In the first place, darkness soon fell over the scene, and secondly, the sight of a notebook and pencil would have stopped the flow of stories instantly. But the listener had a wonderfully retentive memory in which to stow away the anecdotes, and probably only a few of them were lost.

He even enlisted some of his friends among the younger generation of Negroes. They picked up some new ones here and there, scrawled them on scraps of paper, and sent them to him, signing the notes just "Jim" or "Buck." One had evidently been reading the published tales, for he began his letter, "Mr. Harris, I have one tale of Uncle Remus that I have not seen in print yet. . . ."

Some of the stories garnered thus were in the second volume, *Nights with Uncle Remus,* which appeared in 1883, and brought their writer still greater renown. He had some funny correspondence with the publishers over this book.

"I hear that you are going to charge $3 for the volume," he wrote in consternation. "This won't do. The public may

This brought shouts of laughter from the audience.

stand for $2 for the trash, but I doubt it unless you make the cover very interesting and romantic, so to speak."

And so they did; they put palmetto and coconut trees upon it! The author remarked in whimsical despair that because Georgia was a Southern state, Northern people thought of it as being in the very heart of the tropics. As a matter of fact, he informed them, the forests of middle Georgia differ very little from those of New England.

After this book had been out for quite a while, he ended a letter to the publishers with the meek question, "Is there anything coming to me?" There have been some thousands of dollars which came from that little book since then.

Meanwhile, he had been writing for the magazines, stories of other kinds—tragic, pathetic, or humorous, of Georgia life before and after the Civil War. Many had Negroes as prominent characters. Some were stories in a new field—that of the white people of the north Georgia mountains, of whom he wrote with deep understanding and humor.

In the summer of 1882 he made his first visit to New York, with Captain Howell as traveling companion. It is amusing now to read an itinerary which Robert Underwood Johnson, editor of the *Century Magazine* sent him as a suggestion for "seeing New York." It began:

1. Ride down Broadway from Delmonico's on top of stage and ask driver to point out things. A cigar would arrange it with him.

2. Visit Tribune building. Introduce yourself by inclosed card to Mr. Lyman.

3. Walk to Astor House and on down Broadway to Equitable building. Go to top of elevator for view of city

He stealthily packed his bag. He left a note saying,
"I am going home."

and vicinity (bay, rivers, Brooklyn, Jersey City, Staten Island, and the Narrows).

And so on, to Trinity Church, Wall Street, Castle Garden, and the Battery. Point 6 was "Ocean Steamer. For 25c, a sailor will show you over a steamer. Try to find one of the new, big ones." A drive through Central Park and a walk and ride down Fifth Avenue, past the Vanderbilt homes and St. Patrick's Cathedral were further suggestions.

Editors and literary folk offered the two Southerners many courtesies. A dinner for them was given at the Tile Club. Howell had to use much persuasion to induce his friend to go. Joel made himself very popular with those immediately around him at the dinner, although he could not be induced to make a speech or tell a story.

The *Century Magazine* editors arranged another dinner for the two, and one of them, calling at the hotel, procured a promise from Howell that they would both attend, Harris being out sightseeing. Joel suspected that another and perhaps a more vigorous effort was going to be made to wring a speech from him. He grew more and more terrified at the thought, and on the very day of the banquet he stealthily packed his bag, left a note for the captain, saying, "I am going home," stole out of the hotel, and caught a train.

"Hang it! Why did you go back on us so?" wrote Mark Twain, who was a guest at the dinner.

To which Joel replied in part: ". . . When I reflected that probably Mr. Osgood was prepared to put me through a similar experience in Boston, I thought it would be better to come home and commit suicide rather than murder a number of worthy gentlemen by making an ass of myself."

He had now become prominent enough to be teased by Eugene Field, the Chicago columnist, one of whose favorite ways of making fun was to write preposterous stories about eminent persons. This was Field's first shot at him:

Joel C. Harris has had a strangely romantic career. His father was a missionary, and it was at the small town of Booghia, on the South Coast of Africa, that Joel was born. He was educated by his father and acquired a wonderful acquaintance with foreign languages. He is an adept Sanskrit scholar and is deeply versed in Hebraic and Buddhist literature. The sweetly quaint legend of Indian and Judean mythology have found their way into his simple Southern tales, and the spirit of his philosophy is identical with the teaching of Moses and Buddha.

Evidently Eugene had read some of the yarns told by Joel's old tormentor, the poet-preacher, herald of the egg-shaped earth, for another item read:

Joel Chandler Harris, the Southern dialectician and *literateur,* sails for Africa in December, it being his purpose to revisit the little coast town of Joel, where he was born of missionary parents January 13, 1842. Mr. Harris lost a leg in the battle of Lookout Mountain. His career has been full of incidents.

Field then went on airily to declare that Harris was the richest American author, and that the fortune gained by his writings had been invested largely in railway stock, in the *Atlanta Constitution,* and in some of the finest timber land in the South. Joel had enjoyed the joking enormously up to this point, but when people believed the yarn about the fortune and began writing begging letters—one man even asked for five dollars to help pay for his father's tombstone—it didn't seem quite so funny.

CHAPTER TWENTY

By the Living-Room Fire

THE new home out at West End was christened "Snap-Bean Farm"—a joking parody on the name, "Sabine Farm," which Eugene Field had given to his own home, and which in turn was taken from that of the ancient Roman poet, Horace. Snap-Bean Farm was the home of Uncle Remus for the rest of his life. There all his children grew to manhood and womanhood.

There the first daughter died in 1882 when she was less than three years old, and a second daughter, christened Lillian, was born in the same year. Then another little boy, Linton, was born, but lived to be only nine before he died of diphtheria, prostrating the family with grief, for he was greatly beloved.

The place was really something of a farm. There were three cows and many chickens, and in the garden the farmer boasted to his friends one season of having raised a hundred and seventeen bushels of sweet potatoes. His old playmate, Charlie Leonard, who always declared that Joel hated work, said when he heard the name of the place, "Snap-Bean Farm, huh? I bet he hasn't got more than two rows of beans."

The farmer had his troubles with that garden pest known as Johnson grass, but to his whimsical mind it merely suggested "a truly gifted set of dialect verses, beginning, 'La, Mr. Johnson! is dat yo' grass? Well, I done found sump'n you owns at las'! Des take it and go, and don't gimme no sass.'" But he went no farther with the poem.

There were always some happy-go-lucky Negro employees scattered about the place, working in the house and garden and elsewhere. Big, good-natured Chloe walked two miles from her home, morning and evening, to do the milking, and as the years went on, one or two of her numerous sons were usually employed as house boy or yard boy. They furnished much amusement for their employer —especially Rufus, whose job it was for sometime to answer the doorbell. In a letter to one of his daughters when she was at boarding school, the father, remarking that everything around home was about as usual, added, "Rufus persists in going to the door with his breeches rolled up."

At one time when they lost their cook, Chloe came over to handle the kitchen for a few days, and, as usual, brought several of her numerous family with her. "You know Mattie is gone," wrote her employer to his daughter Lillian. "Well, Chloe and her family are cooking for us. The greater part of last week we had in the kitchen Chloe, Lizzie, Ed, Rufus, Johnson, and the mule and wagon."

It was nearly three years before the Harrises felt able to undertake a general remodeling and enlarging of the new home, to bring it nearer to their heart's desire and accommodate their growing family. The plans were drawn, and early in the summer, Mrs. Harris took the children to

Canada to visit her parents—for Captain La Rose's boat had been wrecked below Savannah, and he had gone back to his Canadian farm to live—while her husband superintended the building.

When they returned in the autumn, the new house was all ready, and its master was worn thin with the job. He had built for himself a little study on the upper floor, and there he had a long writing table made, so high that he had to stand or sit at it on a tall bookkeeper's stool. The funny thing was that the table sloped up so steeply that it looked somewhat like one of those cases at which he used to set type.

Another odd thing was that after all this preparation and expense, he found he could not work satisfactorily in that upper room, so far from the family. So the study became an attic storeroom, and he continued to scribble in the bedroom or on a tiny table in the sitting room. His writing nearly all had to be done in the evening, for he still held his place on the *Constitution*.

He could write comfortably only with a pencil. "A pen cramps both my thoughts and my hand," he once told an editor. The typewriter then was a very imperfect machine and still something of a curiosity. For more than twenty years after the birth of Uncle Remus, every manuscript sent by Author Harris to magazine and book editors was written with pencil on huge sheets of copy paper—the wood-pulp stuff on which newspapermen scribbled their work—twelve by eighteen inches in size. His large, shapely script was as easy for most printers to read as typewriting.

His writing and his correspondence became more arduous. He was asked to do an article on "Plantation Music" for *The Critic,* and created a sensation with it. One

of the popular forms of entertainment of that day was what
was called Negro minstrels, in which a troupe of white men
blacked their faces with burned cork and gave what they
believed to be imitations of Negro music and dialect. In
such affairs the Negroes were always shown using the
banjo, tambourine, and bones rattled between the fingers.
Whenever artists drew pictures of Negroes merrymaking
on the plantation, the banjo always appeared.

But now Joel Harris threw a bombshell into the orthodox
belief by writing:

> I have never seen a plantation Negro play it. I have heard
> them make sweet music with the quills—Pan's pipes; I have
> heard them play passingly well on the fiddle, the fife and
> the flute; and I have heard them blow a tin trumpet with
> surprising skill; but I have never seen a banjo, or a tambou-
> rine or a pair of bones, in the hands of a plantation Negro.

What a stew this created! Fixed notions are strong, and
many people rushed into print to say that this fellow
Harris didn't know what he was talking about. But some
Southerners came to his support, notably George W. Cable,
who said that he had seen Negroes singing and dancing
to the music of the banjo in Louisiana—adding, however:
"But it is possible that Mr. Harris never saw a Negro
with one. It is a fact that where you find one Negro with
a banjo, you find a hundred with a fiddle."

There were other troubles, too, he found, which arose
from being a successful author. People came to him for
literary advice, begging him to read the amateurish manuscripts and even to give them introductions to editors.

Squirm as he would, Joel was too good-natured, too sympathetic to be gruff with these people and refuse their requests.

To one young woman living in the north Georgia hills, whose work showed promise, he wrote long letters, advising care in rewriting and polishing her stories, and urging her to remember also that what is really great in literature is the commonplace. His advice was so valuable to her that she later sold some stories to the *Century* and other of the better magazines.

Another woman had some poetry to sell, and wanted him to give her a letter of introduction to an editor. Much against his will he gave her a letter to Mr. Alden of *Harper's*, but immediately wrote Alden an amusing little letter in which he said:

> One of the miseries of my position is that people hereabouts think I have great influence because of the accidental success of the "Remus" trash, and I am constantly embarrassed in that way. All this, however, is no excuse for troubling you, and I write to explain and to beg your pardon. There was no escape for me.

The stories which he had now begun to write about the poor white people of Georgia, both in the mountains and in the lower country, won much praise. "Mingo," the first of them, one of the best of all his stories, appeared in *Harper's* and was such a success that the author planned others.

He and some of his fellow workers on the *Constitution* were sitting in the office one day talking about book titles, and they remarked that some of the greatest and most

popular works in English literature just had the name of
their principal characters for their titles.

"There's *David Copperfield* by Dickens, *Ivanhoe* by Sir
Walter Scott, *Pendennis* by Thackeray—"

"*Adam Bede* by George Eliot," put in another.

A third man picked up a directory of the state of Georgia
and opened it at random. A smile came to his face.

"Now, here's a queer name," he said, "Teague Poteet!
Could anybody's imagination beat that? If you were to
make that the title, people would read the yarn just to find
out what the queer words meant."

"Sounds as if it might be the name of a moonshiner,"
was another's remark, "like the old fellow those deputies
killed—the ones they're trying now." This was a celebrated
case in Atlanta and everybody knew about it.

Already the seed was taking root in Joel's brain. Slowly
the story shaped itself. When he sent it under the title,
"At Teague Poteet's," to Mr. Gilder, the editor of the
Century, he wrote, "Enclosed you will find a sort of
whatshisname. I'm afraid it is too episodical. . . . Perhaps
something else is the matter. If you don't find it available,
you can at least give me some helpful suggestion."

But Mr. Gilder liked it, and bought it. Two years later
this story together with "Mingo" and two others appeared
in book form under the title *Mingo*. The author, sending
a copy to a friend, wrote:

> I have no right to attack you in this manner, but you are
> not defenseless—you are not bound to read it. Indeed it is
> not a book for young men. It is intended to please the aged
> and the half wits of our time—those who are suffering from
> want of sleep.

In 1885 Major J. B. Pond, noted lecture promoter, thought it would be a great idea for Uncle Remus to go on the lecture platform and read some of his own stories.

"The people, including the children, are calling for you," he wrote, "and that has not happened to any other author of recent years. *No* will not do for an answer."

Thomas Nelson Page, the Virginia novelist, also made the suggestion that he and Mr. Harris tour together. But neither proposal interested him. Later Major Pond telegraphed him:

Will give you ten thousand for season tour with James Whitcomb Riley and Mark Twain.

Again the answer was no. To an Atlantic friend he remarked, "I would not even put on a dress suit every night in the winter for ten thousand dollars, much less go on a stage and make a fool of myself."

It was about this time that he wrote a short story which —wonderful to tell!—even he thought was good. He called it "Free Joe and the Rest of the World." It is the story of a Negro in Georgia before the war, one who had been freed by his master and whose condition was even worse than that of the slaves; it moves rapidly to a tragic end. The story is told tersely and without sentimentality, and yet it is one of the most poignant and pathetic of all stories. Its author always thought it the best thing he had ever done, and he was right. It is one of the great short stories of English literature. President Theodore Roosevelt more than once remarked, "In my opinion, the two finest American stories are 'Free Joe' and 'The Man Without a Country.'"

This story was published in 1887 along with four others

in a volume under the title *Free Joe and Other Georgia Sketches*—a little book which contains some of his finest work. "Trouble on Lost Mountain" was the best fiction he ever wrote about the north Georgia hill folk. The other two, "Little Compton" and "Aunt Fountain's Prisoner" were fine examples of Joel Harris's efforts to heal ill feeling between the North and the South.

There was an incident back of "Little Compton," too. One day late in 1885 the telegraph editor handed Joel a slip of paper with the remark, "Something from your old home town." Joel's face grew sad as he read it:

> Sidney C. Prudden, for forty years postmaster at Eatonton, died suddenly last night, at midnight of the day on which his term of office expired. He had just been displaced by President Cleveland in favor of ...

The rest of the dispatch didn't matter. Joel stared through a window at the distant blue hump of Stone Mountain, but he did not see it. He was looking back through the years to the time when kindly Postmaster Prudden, violating the postal laws and regulations, let a poor little redheaded boy read newspapers addressed to other people and thereby gave him a start on his career.

And now Mr. Prudden had collapsed and died because the post office, which, through forty years, had come to be the very breath of life to him, had been taken away from him. Most of the people in Putnam County had been his good friends, but there had been a few who cherished a grudge at him, simply because he was born in New England. A woman whose husband had been killed in the Civil War used to tell her only child, a boy, "When you git old enough, I want you to take your daddy's gun and go to town and kill the first Yankee you see; and ef you don't see no others, go in that thar post office and shoot old Sid Prudden."

But he never did. Passions slowly subsided after the war, and Mr. Prudden lived on, in the country and among the people he had made his own.

Slowly an idea was being born in the storyteller's brain: A Yankee merchant in Georgia during the Civil War . . .

"Little Compton" was the result. Something of Mr. Prudden's character went into that of Compton, but, of course, a romantic story had to be built up, and Joel had trouble in shaping it.

"For several months," he wrote to the *Century* editors, "I have been suffering with fatty degeneration of the mind —and local politics." He was referring to a hot editorial campaign in Atlanta which kept him editorially busy, for he was still on the *Constitution* and doing his other writing in the evening.

When the first draft of "Little Compton" was sent to Mr. Gilder, he suggested some revisions in it, which its author very humbly carried out.

"Your letter in regard to its weak points paralyzed me," he wrote, "but I have tried hard to profit by every suggestion you made. I know that it is much better now, but I do not know whether you will find it available."

But on another story in this book, entitled "Azalea," the modest writer for once rose up and did battle with the editors in behalf of his own ideas, and won. He could be very firm when he thought he was right.

In 1889 another book came from the press—*Daddy Jake the Runaway and Short Stories Told After Dark*. Some of the stories in the volume had been appearing in the *Youth's Companion* and *Saint Nicholas,* the two favorite magazines for young people in those years.

The quantity of work that he was able to do in those evenings at home is astonishing. Yet there was nothing hurried or slipshod about it. He once showed an interviewer sixteen attempts—all discarded—to write the first paragraph of a certain story in a way that would satisfy himself. Even after a story was written and praised by editors, critics, and the public, he frequently continued to be dissatisfied with it. "If it isn't trash from the word go, then I don't know what trash is," he said of one successful story.

Now he had a happy inspiration. He began writing the story of his three years at Turnwold, but began it with a little of his life at Eatonton. He called himself Joe Maxwell in the story, and put in just enough fiction, as he thought, to make the thing more interesting. Mr. Turner, his first great teacher and inspirer, appeared in it under his real name and just as he was. The book was entitled *On the Plantation*. A syndicate of newspapers paid $2,500 for the serial rights, and then it appeared in book form. Some critics said it was one of the most delightful of Mr. Harris's works.

Just after the title page of the volume came its significant dedication:

TO THE MEMORY OF

JOSEPH ADDISON TURNER

LAWYER, EDITOR, SCHOLAR, PLANTER AND PHILANTHROPIST

His gratitude to Mr. Turner was lifelong. Once, when he was at Savannah, the editor of the *Messenger*—a little paper which Eatonton had finally mustered up sufficient enterprise to publish—asked to be permitted to write a sketch of his life. The editor happened to be a brother of J. A. Turner, then six or seven years dead.

Joel agreed to the write-up, saying, "You know me better than I know myself." But he added, "Your brother's great kindness to me must be dwelt upon. I don't think his own children lament him more or will remember him longer. . . ."

CHAPTER TWENTY-ONE

The Wren's Nest

IN THE early years at Snap-Bean Farm, Joel always went home to lunch—or dinner, as it was called in those days and for long afterward in the South. He could have afforded to buy a snack downtown, and it would have taken less time, but he hated to stay away from his family all day, and he much preferred the food he got at home. So he jogged out on the little car line to West End, on which he knew all the drivers—"Dutch" Reynolds, "Grandpa" Bennett, and the rest.

The driver had to eat his noon lunch out of a basket at the end of the line, and there were only a few minutes to do it in. So the distinguished passenger—who did not consider himself at all distinguished—would take the lines and drive the team the last few blocks, while the driver sat inside and ate a bit less hurriedly. If he had not finished his meal by the time they had reached the end of the line, the author would unfasten the doubletrees and, carrying them in one hand, would drive the mules around to the other end of the car, hook them up again, wind the reins around the brake handle, and start home.

244

"Much 'bliged, Mr. Harris," would come in muffled tones from inside the car.

"Much 'bliged, Mr. Harris," would come in muffled tones from inside the car, through a mouthful of cabbage, corn bread, and coffee.

Two more children were born at Snap-Bean Farm—Mildred in 1885 and Joel Chandler Harris, Jr., in 1888. Three of the children having died, there remained four boys and two girls. When the little "J. C.," as they usually called him—later he became "Jake" to the other children—was born, Julian, the eldest, was fourteen. As may be imagined, what with the children and the sunny-dispositioned Negro employees and their children, the place was a beehive of activity, a very genial beehive, where there was much laughter.

Oh yes! and one should add to the turmoil the cows and their calves, the chickens, the ducks, the bees, and the numerous pets—always two or three dogs, cats, a donkey, canaries, pigeons, guinea pigs, rabbits. There was just one hard-and-fast rule about these pets: they must be taken care of kindly and fully. If one was neglected, it could not be kept longer.

Little J. C., as he grew older, took an especial interest in chickens, plain and fancy, and other feathered things. His father in a letter to one of the girls who was away at boarding school, once remarked that "J. C. has an old Langshan rooster that crows 3,431 times a day and his voice can be heard a mile or more."

He very frequently gave news of the animals in letters to the youngsters when they were at school. One of his many playful letters to Lillian—known variously to the family as "Bill," "Billy," "Billy-Ann," and "Miss Pods" (her grandmother's nickname for her)—opened thus:

Dear Miss Billy-Ann:

"Weather cold; wind blowing a gale from the nor'west, thrashing out the roses, and making thin-skinned people feel as if they had lost home and friends and country; old Annabel ailing; calf so poor that it falls down when it tries to bleat; hens deserting their nests, and allowing their eggs to get cold; birds pecking at the strawberries; bucket falling in the well; J. C. cutting a hole in the toe of his Sunday-go-to-meeting shoes; donkey trying to climb the wire fence; pigeons gobbling up the chicken food; apples rotting; stove smoking; drygoods bill heavy; bonnet bill heavier; street-cars behind time; Chloe trying to get in the stove to cook; Rufus dropping plates from the ceiling; milk bill growing; cow-doctor's bill coming in; dust blowing everywhere; kitten getting its tail under the rocking-chair; Brader with his hair soaped smooth on each side; the pony wallowing himself black; planks falling off the fence; Lizzie helping Chloe to harden the biscuit—

Now, how do you suppose I can find any news to write while all this is going on?

The family lost one of its important members in 1891 when Grandmother Harris died. The tie between Joel and his mother had been strong, and he felt her loss very keenly.

As Julian and Lucien—and later Evelyn—grew up into their middle teens and began to go away to academies, and then to visit their grandparents in Canada, their father wrote them long, brotherly letters, usually signing himself "Your affectionate Dad," telling all the news of home and family, giving them advice, but trying hard not to lecture.

These letters and the replies were more intimate and understanding than one usually finds passing between father and sons.

Before he was sixteen, Julian had gotten the idea that he wanted to write—either as an author or as a journalist. He took up the study of shorthand. During a visit of nearly a year to his grandparents in Canada, he attended the Frères Maristes College to improve his French. He began writing descriptions of what he saw in French Canada and sending them to his father, who criticized the pieces and showed him how to improve them. When one of them was finally published in the *Constitution* and praised by the editors, Julian himself could not have been any prouder than his father. The youth came home and found a place on the *Atlanta News* as a cub reporter at seventeen, later going to the *Constitution*.

The father's letters to his sons were full of wisdom. When Lucien, too, went to Canada for a visit, he was in the throes of a love affair with a fine girl in his home neighborhood. His father, who saw the girl frequently, gave him news of her, praised her highly, and exchanged confidences with Lucien about her. The son was so close to his father in spirit that he told him all his hopes and fears, and the father gave him advice and comfort. This love story had a happy ending; three years later Lucien married the young lady.

Along with real home news, his letters to the boys frequently contained bits of the nonsensical gossip which he liked to write to his children, as when he wrote to Lucien of affairs in West End: "The Grigsbys swarming across the lot at meal-time and Mrs. Richardson shooing at your bantam roosters, and J. C. rolling down the woodpile, and the ducks nibbling at the young turnips, and Malsby's baby howling like a freight engine."

A friend of the family said that the Harris children all seemed to an outsider to do as they pleased, and yet there was a sort of order, too, and they all grew up with a very definite sense of duty. Father was indulgent—he believed in having a good time—and yet on points of order he was firm. "This is thusly" he would say when he was laying down the law, and when he said that, it meant business. But he wouldn't curb the children's fun, when it was kept within the bounds of reason. A letter to Lillian gives a comic hint of this:

> You will find it very much like home when you return, with Mama crying out every quarter of an hour—"I'll call your papa if you don't behave!" or "Joel, can't you come to these children?" and then if I make no response, "Your papa says I spoil you, but he's the one that does the spoiling." This last all in one word, as it were. And so we go on raising our children, at a loss whether to pet them or bump their heads together.

Perhaps the pageant of children—his own and others—through his home caused him to think more of children's stories. Anyhow, he now wrote a series of books of a new sort for him; more like fairy stories than anything he had done before, and yet with a lot of the fun and satire of Uncle Remus, too, though they were not told in Negro dialect.

The first of these was *Little Mr. Thimblefinger and his Queer Country,* which appeared in 1894. It seems that Buster John and his sister, Sweetest Susan, were two little children who lived on a farm. They had for a playmate a Negro girl named Drusilla, who was supposed to be a sort of nurse for them, but who was only a little older than they were.

One day when they were down by the spring they saw Mr. Thimblefinger, a little man not more than four inches tall, who lived in the country beyond the spring. He invited them to visit his country. They didn't see how they could pass through the spring without being drowned, but he revealed to them that at precisely nineteen minutes and nine seconds past nine o'clock, the water was as dry as air, and they could pass through it without even getting wet.

So away they went into this strange country, where they became acquainted with Mr. Rabbit and old Miss Meadows and Chickamy Crany Crow and Tickle-My-Toes. Here Mr. Rabbit had become a big, rustic old fellow who sat in a rocking chair and smoked a pipe and did his share of the story telling, but was apt to fall asleep whenever anybody else told one.

These books appeared rapidly. In 1895 there were two, *Mr. Rabbit at home* and *The Story of Aaron*.

In the country beyond the spring the children heard much gossip of the animals—the troubles of Brother Lion and Brother Bear and Mrs. Blue Hen and Mr. Willy Weasel and Miss Mimy Mink and others. But they also heard about those monstrous creatures, the Woog and the Weeze and the Diddypawn, and about Uncle Rain and Brother Drouth. When a little boy went to Uncle Rain's house to complain of too much wet weather, he found the house full of drizzle and mist, but Uncle Rain politely went to a closet and brought out a dry spot for him to sit on. Whereupon the little boy described the sufferings of the people from the rainy season so touchingly that Uncle Rain had to wipe his eyes on a corner of the fog which hung on the towel rack behind the door.

Three more books in this series followed at short intervals: *Aaron in the Wildwoods, Plantation Pageants*—of which its author wrote, "Glancing back over its pages, it seems to be but a patchwork of memories and fancies, a confused dream of old times"—and *Wally Wanderoon*. Wally was a new character in the series, one who was always looking for the good old times. He finally found a relic of those times, an "old-fashioned" story telling machine. He set it going for Buster John and Susan and Drusilla, and it ground out some delightful tales.

Meanwhile, great and momentous events were taking place in the Harris family. In December 1895 Lucien was married to Alleen, the charming girl about whose attitude he had been so worried when he was in Canada three years before. It was the first wedding among the children; and "children," indeed, these two seemed to Papa and Mama Harris, for Lucien was only twenty, though already a very capable young businessman. Papa suffered the usual agony of embarrassment at the wedding because of having to dress up and be stared at by so many people. He vanished immediately after the ceremony, and was later found sitting contentedly in an alcove, hidden by portieres.

Out of the southwestern corner of the little "farm" he cut a lot and gave it to Lucien, and the son built his home there. In the following year, Julian was married, and he was given a lot on the northwest corner. And so the process went on. Evelyn and J. C. as they married, settled on lots between their two older brothers—the system continued, even after the father's death—and the two daughters, upon their marriage, received lots on the front edge of the property, alongside the parental home. Thus was completed a family group the like which it would be hard to find elsewhere. But the last few gifts had to be made by Mother, for before the younger children married, beloved Daddy was gone.

A year after Lucien's marriage came another exciting event—the birth of the first grandchild. "He seems to be about 81 years old," wrote his grandfather to Lillian, "but he will get considerably younger in a few days."

In another letter he said:

> You remember I told you he is very old. Well, it's a fact. He is bald-headed and all his teeth have dropped out, and his head is wobbly and he's too decrepit to walk. And he's irritable, too, just like an old man. He sleeps most of the time and that is another sign of extreme old age; he can hold nothing in his hands. He may grow younger as he grows older, and I hope he will. You said something about my being a grandpa. But the way I look at it, this baby is too small and wrinkled to count. If I'm to be a grandpa, I want to be one, sure enough. I want to be the grandpa of something that you can find without hunting through a bundle of shawls and blankets. . . .

And so, as other babies came to Lucien's and Julian's homes, he continued his joking references to them in his letters to Lillian and Mildred (usually known in the family as "Tommy"). "The kid continues to weep copiously," he wrote of another infant, "from which I conclude that he is of a melancholy, if not despairing disposition. This he must inherit from me."

In 1900, when the South African war was being waged between the British and the Boer republic, and the newspaper reports were full of Dutch words, he began a letter to Mildred thus:

My Dear Dr. Delion:

Your esteemed favor of open date and current month has been received at the Laager now occupied by those notorious Boers, the Harrises. The Kopje on which the Laager is situated is the same as ever. People who reach it by the nearest route still have to trek across three Veldts and climb three terraced Kopjes. The various and sundry Kleiner Kidjs of the Harris tribe were alive and kicking and also squalling at last account. . . .

But his letters to the girls were not all fun. There were streaks of serious advice and wisdom in them. Once when Lillian was vexed because the convent school authorities would not let her exchange letters with a fine boy, so well known in the Harris home that he was, as her father said, "almost like one of the family," he wrote her that "You know perfectly well that we have no objection to your corresponding with him. Yet at the school it is a different matter. We as well as you must be governed by the rules." So if the Sisters thought it advisable that her mind be not diverted by correspondence with a young man, that, he decreed, must be the last word on the subject.

Another important Snap-Bean event of the middle 1890's must not be overlooked. Someone went to the mail box at the gate one spring morning and found that a pair of wrens had decided to set up housekeeping there. They had already brought in some hay as a foundation.

"We must make other arrangements for mail," said Father at once to the family and to the postman. "We must not break up a home."

He wrote a little magazine piece about the incident a year or two later. After that, he liked to speak of the home, not as Snap-Bean Farm, but "At the Sign of the Wren's Nest." And so it remains to this day.

CHAPTER TWENTY-TWO

A Path to His Door

NEARLY every evening his pencil was busy, at the living-room table, or at the little one in his bedroom, so small that it could barely hold the big sheets of copy paper. Collections of his short stories which had been appearing in newspapers and magazines appeared between cloth covers at frequent intervals. *Balaam and His Master,* a volume containing six tales of Georgia, before and during the Civil War, was one of these.

A year later, in 1892, appeared *Uncle Remus and His Friends,* some more fables and a number of poems in Negro dialect, which he had been writing more and more frequently. In his brief introduction to this volume, he said that he was going to leave the question of the origins of the tales "to those who think they know something about it. My own utter ignorance I confess without a pang."

For *Nights With Uncle Remus,* which had appeared only six years before, he had written a forty-three page introduction, all about folklore. He now laughed rather sheepishly at its "enterprising inconsequence" and "unconscious humor." "I knew a good deal more about folklore then," he said, "than I know now. To know that you are

ignorant is a valuable form of knowledge, and I am grad-
ually accumulating a vast store of it."

With this volume of 1892, the author declared that Uncle
Remus was saying farewell to his public; he would speak
no more. Which simply meant that his creator had so
many other ideas buzzing in his brain that he didn't want
to be bothered with the old man any more. But how little
he knew of the future! Uncle Remus wouldn't be
squelched, and the public wouldn't permit it. They kept
calling for him, and he insisted on being heard now and
then.

But during the Nineties some of those other ideas came
pouring from the press; the first novel, for example, *Sister
Jane*. In 1878 he had written a novel, *The Romance of
Rockville,* and it ran serially in the *Constitution*. It wasn't
a good novel, and no one knew this better than its author.
It was never even offered to a book publisher. Now he took
some threads from it and wove them into a new fabric. He
made the central character a strong-minded, true-souled
woman, with a tongue sometimes sharp, but a heart full
of loving kindness. It was to some extent a picture of his
mother, who had died five years before.

Sister Jane in the story had a timid brother, into whom
the author put something of himself. Writing to a friend,
he said:

> Sister Jane is still selling, but it's poor stuff. No doubt
> that's because the brother represents my inner—my inner—
> oh, well! my inner spezerinktum; I can't think of the other
> word. It isn't self, and it isn't—oh, yes! it's the other fellow
> inside of me, the fellow who does all my literary work while
> I get the reputation, being really nothing but a corn-field

journalist. . . . I wish I could trot the other fellow out when company comes. But he shrinks to nothing, and is gone.

Another volume of short stories, *Tales of the Home Folks in Peace and War,* quickly followed this. Here was one author who never had to seek a market. The market sought him. Meanwhile, a new character, Aunt Minervy Ann, had been born—one quite as distinct and delightful as Uncle Remus. The stories about her appeared in *Scribner's Magazine,* and were published in book form in 1899 as *The Chronicles of Aunt Minervy Ann.* Vigorous and even violent with her tongue—yes, and with her hands, too, when it seemed necessary to her, but true-hearted and loyal to her "white folks," she had some fascinating tales to tell of life in middle Georgia before and after the war.

There were evident traces of Chloe, long a faithful servant at the Wren's Nest, in Aunt Minervy Ann. But old Forsyth acquaintances insisted that she was Aunt Sallie, the Harrisons' cook, who had later gone with them to Atlanta, and who called on "Marse Joe" at the *Constitution* office now and then, to swap reminiscences with him and laugh so loudly that she could be heard all over the place.

Maybe he was talking about one of Sallie's calls when he said to a friend one day, "Aunt Minervy Ann's getting mighty restless. She came in here just now and sat down in that chair and began telling me a story about Mis' Jones's pa'sol. I've got to be writing something about Aunt Minervy Ann." But it is more likely that he was just talking about the imaginary Aunt Minervy. His dream characters became very real to him. This is seen in a memorandum which he once began to write—why or for whom we do not know:

Sister Jane was written

1. To get rid of a number of people—critics call them characters, but to me they are people—who were capering about in my mind.
2. To take out of the mouth of my mind the bad taste of some pessimistic books I had re

There it breaks off. But it has told what we already know, that he disliked pessimism and dirt in literature.

All his life he continued to be the most modest, even bashful, author in history. Once when he was in New York on a business trip, he called at the office of the *Century Magazine,* which was publishing his stories frequently, to see Mr. Johnson, the associate editor. In fact, that was a part of his errand to New York. But two bright young men in the outer office evidently did not know who Mr. J. C. Harris was, and this mild, pudgy, freckled, sleepy-eyed man in the broad-brimmed black felt hat must have looked countrified and unimportant to them. So they told him curtly that Mr. Johnson was busy and could not see him. At that, he meekly bowed himself out and went back to Georgia.

"I know how things are," he wrote later, when Mr. Johnson was apologizing for the error. "I don't want to be bothered when I am busy, and I know how to sympathize with others who live in the channels of botheration."

Once when he and Henry Grady were in New York together, a dinner was arranged for them by the literary folk. The thought of it threw J. C. H. into a perspiration, for he had become such a literary lion that all eyes were upon him whenever he entered a public gathering. As he had done once before, he gave Grady the slip and returned to Atlanta.

His wife, who was not expecting to see him for several days, was riding downtown on a street car when she was startled by a glimpse of a familiar face passing her on an outbound car.

"If I didn't know he was in New York," she told herself, "I'd be sure that was Joel."

So strongly was she impressed by this that she went to the *Constitution* office. "What do you know of my husband's whereabouts?" she asked of Mr. Finch, the managing editor.

"Why, don't you know he is in town?" returned Mr. Finch, surprised. "Haven't you seen him? He came by here a while ago, and went on home."

She hurried home and found her husband contentedly inspecting the flowers on the lawn.

"Joel, why are you back so soon?" she asked, as soon as she caught sight of him.

"Why, aren't you glad to see me?" he asked in mock reproach.

"Of course I am." She kissed him. "But you came back so much sooner than I expected."

"I got so homesick I couldn't stand New York any longer," he told her. "I just had to come home as soon as I could get here."

That was probably as near being the real reason as the other. He always left home reluctantly, and he could never stay away long. Good friends like James Whitcomb Riley and others begged him to come and visit them, but he never went. He received tempting invitations to come to

Europe, where his works were well known, but he turned them down.

"Too far from home," was his reason. "Georgia's good enough for me."

In 1889, when two members of the *Constitution* staff were married to each other at a small town east of Atlanta, the bridegroom persuaded his friend Harris—by what magic or hypnotism no one can guess to this day—to serve as best man. Perhaps it was because this was a small town, and he was at home with small-town folks.

But even in a small town he could not make a speech. No, not even at Eatonton, where Miss Fannie Lee Leverette, daughter of his old neighbor, raised money and organized the first school library that the town had had, naming it in his honor. They thought they had him cornered once, when he was down there at a public affair, sitting on the rostrum with Henry Grady. Grady, who was even a better orator than he was an editor, made the principal address of the evening. Then there were shouts of "Harris! Harris!"

He was appalled—terror-stricken! But desperation gave him strength and wit to rise to the occasion.

"I'm c-coming," he stammered, as he rose to his feet. "I've n-never b-been able to make a public speech without wetting my throat," he continued, as he descended the steps from the rostrum, and started down the aisle among them. "So you must excuse me until I get a drink." They laughed and applauded, but watched him uncertainly as he passed out through the rear door. Then it began to dawn upon them that he had escaped—he was gone for good!

Those were the only remarks he ever made to a public gathering.

In Atlanta he was even shyer. He was persuaded to go
to a party once, and he wrote to one of the girls, "When
I got out, I panted right heartily, and felt as if I had
done a day's ploughing."

When the silver wedding anniversary of Captain Howell
and his wife approached, they planned a reception. But the
captain said to his old friend, "Joe, we have decided that
we can't have this affair unless you come to it."

"Oh, I can't do it! I can't!" he protested. "You know
I never go to parties—" But Howell was equally determined.

"Why, man, this is our silver wedding," he urged. "It's
a great occasion. We'll never have another one. All our
best friends *must* be there. . . ."

But he was making no progress at all until Mrs. Howell
took a hand. "Surely you wouldn't refuse *me,* would you
Joe?" she asked pleadingly. "I couldn't feel happy if you
weren't there."

He looked at her beseechingly, but his resistance weak-
ened. At last he gave in. "Yes, I'll come."

It was such an unusual distinction that the Howells
couldn't resist telling everybody that Joe Harris was coming to the reception. That promised to increase the at-
tendance. The whole town was agog. On the afternoon
of the eventful day, Captain Howell, just to make sure,
dropped around to check up on him. Yes, his wife said,
he was going to go through with it. And there were his
best clothes, all ready and laid out on the bed.

He put them on after supper, and he and Essie walked
through the vacant lots and clumps of trees to the Howell
home. It was brilliantly lighted, and as they neared it,
they heard the murmur of voices and laughter. Joel's cour-

age oozed out of him. He simply couldn't go in, to be gazed at and fussed over as the chief guest of the evening.

"You go in," he told his wife. "I just can't."

She did not argue much with him; she knew him too well. "But how am I to get home?" she finally asked.

"I'll come back in a couple of hours and whistle for you."

And that was that. She watched the clock, donned her wraps at the appointed time, went outside and found her faithful swain hovering in the shadows, waiting for her.

But with a few friends of long standing, who treated him as one of themselves, he was the merriest of companions. By the middle Nineties, the West End streetcar line had been extended past his place and electrified. As he wrote, "The cars run gaily and frequently until the company is scared by a thunderstorm." But still they ran so far apart that patrons knew their schedule, and it was disastrous to miss one. Author Harris, Captain Howell, Frank L. Stanton, and three or four other close friends in the neighborhood would go downtown on the same car every morning, and to other passengers within earshot it sounded like a session of the Gridiron Club. Many a man along the line gulped the last of his breakfast coffee standing and ran two or three blocks, rather than miss "Joe Harris's car" and the jokes and stories which kept it in a roar all the way downtown.

This different writer was also at his best with a close friend or two on a winter evening before the living-room fire, which he loved to poke and stir, or on the broad porch on a summer night, while tree toads chirruped and mockingbirds sang in the tulip tree by the steps. It was thus that he sat through a memorable fortnight with James Whitcomb Riley in 1900.

Nearly twenty years before that, the Indiana poet, then a young journalist, had first written of his admiration for Uncle Remus—who, in turn, became an admirer of Mr. Riley's poetry. But it was not until 1900 that they met. Then Mr. Riley came down for a two weeks' visit to the Wren's Nest, and endeared himself to the whole family. He and Joel Harris were natural cronies from the start. They went to the post office together, went out to the parks and to vaudeville shows, but many afternoons and evenings they just sat on the porch, trading literary opinions, or preferably stories and laughter, or sometimes, as "Jim" put it, just "shut clean to, a sayin' nothin' 'cause we don't haf to." When the guest departed, he left such a void behind him that his host wrote to Mildred, "Your Unc. Jeems has done gone and went, and the house feels as if all the furniture had been taken out."

Now the host of the Wren's Nest had become so famous that many of the great ones of earth were writing to him or beating a path to his door. Joaquin Miller, "the Poet of the Sierras," Dr. Lyman Abbott, Walter Hines Page, Andrew Carnegie, and many other noted folk were among the visitors to the unpretentious home at West End. Mr. Carnegie's first words, as he shook hands with Uncle Remus, were, "How's Sis' Cow?"

"Po'ly," was the reply.

With these people, who knew how to meet him on his own ground, he unbent and was his real self. But when some "lion hunter" journeyed out to his home to rhapsodize over him and have the honor of shaking his hand, the caller might not get a dozen words out of him during the whole interview.

CHAPTER TWENTY-THREE

Uncle Remus Tells His Last Story

BY 1899 there were Harris stories appearing in *The Saturday Evening Post;* some of them famous ones. "Why the Confederacy Failed" and "The Kidnapping of President Lincoln" were probably the two best. Their author also wrote editorials for the *Post.* A collection of the stories appeared in book form in 1900 under the title, *On the Wing of Occasions.*

In some of these stories a noted character, Billy Sanders, a rustic philosopher supposed to be from Shady Dale, Georgia, made his appearance, and his homely wit and wisdom were so popular that his creator was asked to write a series of Billy Sanders opinions on life and current events for the new magazine, *The World's Work.* Billy continued to talk for the next eight years. Once he even changed the name of a town!

It was a funny little instance of small-town sensitiveness. An imaginary hamlet called Harmony Grove was described in one of the articles as a quiet, unpretentious little place, but there was no thought of reproach in the description, for Joel Harris loved that sort of community.

It happened, however, that there was really a town of

She called on Marse Joe at the Constitution *office to swap stories with him.*

that name in Georgia, and it was enormously offended. "A casual reader," wrote one indignant citizen, "would think Harmony Grove a regular Sleepy Hollow, or a little cross-roads town with no get-up-and-get-about it, instead of being as it is to-day the best town of its size in Georgia." Shortly after that, the town even changed its name to Commerce, much to the distress of the gentle soul back of Billy Sanders.

Offers were now coming thick and fast. In 1900 Mr. Harris was asked to accept the editorship of *Everybody's Magazine,* and two book publishing houses wanted to put him on an annual salary and take all his output. He rejected the magazine offer and accepted one of the others, a contract with McClure, Phillips & Company. And with that, he gave up his job on the *Constitution,* after twenty-four years of service.

There had been great changes at the office in that time. His dear friend, Henry Grady, had died eleven years before, and Captain Howell had recently sold out his interest. But there were still close ties with the paper. Son Julian had become—at the age of twenty-four—managing editor, and a little later Evelyn worked up to the job of city editor, though he eventually left journalism to go into the telephone business. Frank L. Stanton, who had been an office boy with the *Savannah News* when young Joel first went to work there, had developed into a poet, and was brought by his old friend up to the *Constitution,* with which he had a connection for the rest of his days.

Twenty-four years of habit cannot be broken off all at once. For a long time, ex-columnist Harris could not resist going down to the *Constitution's* morning editorial conference every day, just as if he belonged there. He even went down on Sundays and holidays and puttered around.

However, he rejoiced in the freedom from routine. "If the greatest position on the round earth were to be offered me," he told a friend, "I wouldn't take it. The responsibility would kill me in two weeks. Now I haven't any care or any trouble, and I have resolved not to worry any more."

With the increased leisure now gained, he wrote his second novel, *Gabriel Tolliver,* into which, he confessed, he put a great deal of himself—and he dedicated it to his good friend, James Whitcomb Riley. He was greatly pleased when "Jamesy," as the poet often signed letters to him, dedicated a new volume of poems to him. These two had another jolly two weeks together at Lithia Springs, Georgia, in 1902.

For worries would come whether he wanted them or not. That visit to the springs was made after a series of illnesses which had attacked him during the previous year, and which left him looking older. He stooped a little more now, which made him seem shorter than ever and more roly-poly, and the red of his hair had dulled a bit.

Evelyn, despite his newspaper responsibilities, was a devoted and efficient secretary during his illness. But even after he was up and about, his hand was so shaky for a time that he gave up writing with pen or pencil and began to tap out his letters and manuscript on a typewriter, using the one-finger-and-hunt system, and now coming down to sheets of paper of ordinary business size.

Because of these periods when he could not write, he insisted upon giving up the contract with McClure, Phillips & Company. He said they should not be compelled to pay him for time when he was too ill to work. But he let them retain the right to publish his books.

Famous visitors continued to tread the trail to the Wren's

Nest, as the nestlings departed one by one. Evelyn was married in 1903, and before long was building his home on the lot carved out of the western edge of the so-called farm—though the neighborhood around it was no longer rural.

A photographer who went down to Atlanta about this time to make some news pictures of the author found in him not only some of the traits of Uncle Remus, "but a good deal of Br'er Rabbit, a pinch of Br'er Fox, more than a suspicion of Br'er 'Possum, a faint trace of Br'er B'ar, and in particular, *all* of the little boy."

He was now becoming somewhat accustomed to this sort of thing and to being interviewed by professional journalists. When Ray Stannard Baker came in one day and said, "Mr. Harris, I want to write you up for the *Outlook*," he laughed, and said:

"That reminds me of Simon Sugg, a queer old chap downstate who was put into fiction by an old acquaintance. I knew him when I was a boy. One day a friend met him and said:

" 'Simon, do you remember Jim Hooper, that went to school with us down at Monticello?'

" 'Oh, Jim Hooper—of co'se I remember Jim. Little slim feller, wa'n't he?'

" 'That's him. Well, Jim's gone and noveled you.'

" 'Noveled me! Has he?' says Simon. 'Well ding his hide!'

"Simon hadn't the faintest idea what Jim had done to him, but he was properly indignant, anyhow."

There had been many requests for more Uncle Remus stories, and from time to time, while he was writing other stories or Billy Sanders articles, he had turned out an Uncle Remus tale for a magazine or put another into rhyme. A volume of the verses, *Tar Baby and Other Rhymes of Uncle Remus,* appeared in 1904, and another volume of the prose stories, *Told by Uncle Remus,* in the following year. "Jamesy" Riley, was so delighted by the appearance of the verses that he wrote a jingle about them, beginning:

> Indianapolis, Indiana
> Leventeen-Hundred-an'-
> Full-er-Fleas.
> Hit's mighty good news er *new* Ol' Uncle Remus Rhymes,
> Which I done prophesyin' 'bout forty-levm times—
> All de whole kit-an-bilin' er de jingles an' de chimes
>   Ol' Uncle orter sing us ef he 'spectin' to redeem us—
>   Remus—
>   Ol' Uncle Remus an' his new-ol' rhymes.
> O, it's "Hi, my rinktum," he 'low one day
> When I tel him dat a ne'r batch er ol' rhymes pay—
> En it's "Ho, my Riley! youer leadin' me erstray.—
>   I taste my last er singin' an' I gwine ter stay absteemus.—
>   Remus—
>   Ol' Uncle Remus tetchin' no mo' rhymes."

One of the greatest admirers of all of the Harris writings was President Theodore Roosevelt. He wrote frequently, expressing his appreciation. He said that when he was a boy, an aunt from Georgia had told him some of the Br'er Rabbit stories. The Roosevelt children, one by one, all acquired autographed copies of Uncle Remus books.

When the President and Mrs. Roosevelt planned to visit Atlanta in 1905, he wrote to Clark Howell, then editor of the *Constitution,* saying that Mrs. Roosevelt could remain in Atlanta only two hours, and asking if it would be possible for her to meet the great author.

"As you know," he concluded, "our entire household is devoted to Joel Chandler Harris."

The request was too important to be refused, but the bashful man's agony as the dread October day approached may be faintly imagined. Just to make sure that there was no slip-up, a committee of prominent citizens escorted him to the railway station. The train arrived, and the beaming Teddy was introduced all around. As they were entering the carriages, he turned to a member of the committee and said, "I'd like for Mr. Harris to ride in the carriage with Mrs. Roosevelt."

"Certainly!" said the committeeman, and turned to look for the author. He had vanished!

"Where is he?" asked the gentleman excitedly. Then someone caught sight of him escaping through the crowd.

"There he goes!" cried a voice.

"Catch him!" shouted another.

There was a rush after him, and the fugitive was hustled back to the carriage, making little resistance now that he was discovered, but redder than any lobster. A little later, the amazing spectacle was presented to Atlantans of Joel Chandler Harris on the balcony of the governor's mansion, along with the governor and President and Mrs. Roosevelt, reviewing a military parade.

He was then compelled to violate another rule; he went to a luncheon given for the visitors. There was no escape. There were speeches afterward, of course, and during his talk the President said:

"I am going . . . to cause for a minute or two acute dis-

UNCLE REMUS AT THE WHITE HOUSE!

Cartoon in the "Constitution," November 19, 1907

comfort to a man of whom I am very fond. . . . Georgia has done a great many things for the Union, but has never done more than when she gave Joel Chandler Harris to American literature. . . ."

It was secretly very gratifying to the blushing, suffering man, who sat with his eyes on his plate; he loved it. The only question was whether he would be able to live through the embarrassment of it.

Next, the Roosevelts wanted him to visit the White House. Not until two years later was this accomplished, and even then only with the aid of Julian, who went along as moral support. The Roosevelt children greeted him first, and that put him more at ease. There was only one other guest at dinner, another Southerner, General Fitzhugh Lee. With these understanding people the bashful man was soon at home, and the evening was a lively one. When he departed next morning, the family agreed that they had never had a more delightful guest.

He put some of his impressions of the White House and its occupants into the mouth of Billy Sanders, who was supposed to have made a call there.

"It's a home," said Billy. "It'll come over you like a sweet dream the minnit you git in the door. . . . To make it all more natchal, a little boy was in the peazzer, waitin' to see me, an' what more could you ax than that a little boy should be waitin' for to see you before he was tucked in bed."

The little boy was Quentin Roosevelt, who, as an American aviator, gave his life eleven years later in the first World War.

The acclaim of the Roosevelts was only a small part of a world-wide chorus. When Rudyard Kipling learned in 1895 that one of his *Jungle Books* had been praised by the

Harris whom he admired so much, he wrote to him, "This makes me feel some inches taller in my boots; for my debt to you is of long standing."

He went on to tell how "Uncle Remus and the sayings of the noble beasties ran like wildfire through an English public school when I was about fifteen. . . . And six years ago in India, meeting an old schoolmate of those days, we found ourselves quoting whole pages of 'Uncle Remus' that had got mixed in with the fabric of the old school life."

A group of Southerners were dining in a club in London with some English acquaintances, including a few noblemen, when some one of the Americans mentioned Atlanta.

"Atlanta!" came a quick chorus from the Englishmen. "That's where Uncle Remus lives."

An English critic wrote that the Uncle Remus stories were as well known in England as *Aesop's Fables. Punch* and other English papers adapted the tales to political caricature. In Australia, the volumes were always in stock in the bookstores. And back they went to the English-speaking colonies in Africa, from which great continent they had come. A tourist in Egypt told of seeing a group of children around a story teller, who was relating the Uncle Remus tales to them in their own language. The stories were translated and published in France and Germany, and into Bengali for use in India. A Chinese ambassador who had enjoyed them sent a "smoke tree" to be planted in the yard of the Wren's Nest.

The University of Pennsylvania wanted to confer a doctor's degree on the author, but the thought of standing on a rostrum before hundreds of people, togged out in a long gown and listening to a eulogy of himself, was too much for him. This university is one which stipulates that to re-

ceive such a degree, you must come to get it—and so bashful
Uncle Remus did not get it. A Georgia college, Emory,
gave him the degree of Doctor of Literature, however, and
was good enough to confer it in his absence and send the
diploma to him.

It was in 1905 that Julian conceived the idea of a Southern magazine, with his father as editor in chief. Some Atlanta men connected with the *Constitution* and others were
interested, but they had difficulty in persuading the elder
Harris to like the idea of a publication called *Uncle
Remus's Magazine,* to be edited by himself. At last he gave
in. But the preparations dragged along over several months,
and it was not until March 1907 that the first number appeared. President Roosevelt was one of the first subscribers,
and, of course, old comrade Riley was asked to be one of
the first contributors.

Julian was managing editor, and there was a young man
on the staff named Don Marquis, later one of the most
famous of New York columnists, but who wrote articles
both grave and gay, and some amusing poetry for *Uncle
Remus's Magazine.*

The editor in chief wrote a long editorial for each number, always referring to himself as "the Farmer"; and there
were frequent musings by Billy Sanders, occasional poems,
and now and then an Uncle Remus story. One of the last
things he wrote starts off with a charming picture of the
home life of Br'er Bar:

"He had a son name' Simmon an' a gal name' Sue, not
countin' his ol' 'ooman, an' dey all live wid one an'er day
atter day and night atter night; an' when one on 'em went
abroad, dey'd be 'spected home 'bout meal-time if not befo';
an' dey segashuated right along f'm day to day, washin' der

face an' han's in de same wash-pan on de back po'ch an' wipin' on de same towel, same as all happy famblies allers does. . . ."

The magazine throve greatly from the start. But its editor was now failing. Even when it was being organized, he confessed to his friends that he was feeling his age. In the spring of 1908 his wife noticed that he seemed to be losing interest in the flowers and the vegetable garden. He spent less time at his office, and frequently lay upon the couch in the living room for an hour or so—a thing unusual with him. He ended a two-year correspondence, one of the sort he loved, with a little schoolgirl in Wisconsin whom he had never seen, but who wrote so well that he had suggested that she write something for the magazine.

For a long time he would not see a doctor, but at last consented to have one called in. By that time, even an operation proved to be of no avail. He himself decided that this illness was his last. Although he was not an irreligious man, yet he had never been a member of any church. He had for some years past thought of entering the Catholic Church, in which his children had been reared. One day during his illness a priest, Father Jackson, an old friend of the family, called at the house. The sick man sent for him and asked that he be baptized and confirmed, which was speedily done.

He grew steadily worse. All America was concerned over his illness, and letters and telegrams were pouring in. Among those who wrote most anxiously was President Roosevelt. Only two or three days before the end, one of the letters from Teddy was read to the dying man. He smiled faintly and said, "The President has been very kind."

On the night of July 2, 1908, while the tree toads and mockingbirds, all unconscious of the impending tragedy, sang in the trees about the house, Atlanta was already mourning, for it was believed that the end was at hand. During the following forenoon, one of his sons came in and said, "How do you feel now, Father?"

With a flicker of his old humor, he murmured, "Just about the tenth part of a gnat's eyebrow better."

Then he lost consciousness, and never spoke again. Just as the sun was setting, Buster John and Sweetest Susan and Drusilla and his other dream children took him by the hand and led him into the country beyond the spring.

Over his grave has been placed an enormous boulder of Georgia granite, and upon a bronze tablet let into its side you may read a part of his foreword to a special edition of Uncle Remus tales, issued during his latter years, when illness and sorrow had begun to have their effect upon his blithe spirit:

I seem to see before me the smiling faces of thousands of children—some young and fresh and some wearing the friendly marks of age—but all children at heart, and not an unfriendly face among them. And while I am trying hard to speak the right word, I seem to hear a voice lifted above the rest, saying, "You have made some of us happy." And so I feel my heart fluttering and my lips trembling, and I have to bow silently and turn away and hurry back into the obscurity that suits me best.

Afterword

ON A MEMORABLE afternoon I went out to the Wren's Nest, now maintained as a memorial to Joel Chandler Harris; I saw the trees he planted —the fine magnolia, the big tulip tree by the steps, of which he once said, "I'd like this tree to be my monument"; the giant wistaria vine sheltering the old boxed-in well, over which hangs the pulley whereby the water used to be raised; saw his rocking chair on the broad porch, the living room, once so merry, the tables there and in the bedroom where he worked, his old Hammond typewriter with the wooden case on the one in the bedroom, his broad-brimmed black felt hat, the last one he wore, beside it; the dining room with all the original furnishings, where there must have been some jolly mealtimes forty or fifty years ago; the fringe of cottages around two rims of the farm, which were the children's first homes when they married, and from which they have all long since flown.

And there in the visitors' book were the names not only of prominent Americans, but of others, such as Charles bring back the past with peculiar vividness, was about a hundred feet of old zigzag rail fence from Turnwold; the rails, like elderly men and women, worn thin and frail by seventy-five years of storm and stress, for many of them

277

were there when young Joel was setting type in the printing shop, and he may have scrambled over them when he went hunting with Jim-Poke Gaither.

Out at Emory University there are still older relics: the old blank book whose pages contain his first literary efforts; his little school composition on "The Elephant," written at the age of nine, his first book, the *Life of General Taylor,* given to him when he was five. And there are a file of *The Countryman,* the silver watch given to him by Papa La Rose at the time of his wedding, the Japanese netsuke charm added to it by Mrs. Theodore Roosevelt, his pencil, pen, and typewritten manuscripts, letters, and many other things.

I am greatly indebted to Mr. Lucien Harris and his brothers and sisters for aid in the preparation of this book; also to Dr. Thomas H. English, curator of the Joel Chandler Harris Collection at Emory University for information, assistance, and counsel; to Miss Margaret Jemison, the University librarian; to Miss Fannie Lee Leverette, daughter of those kindly neighbors of little Joel and his mother at Eatonton; to Mrs. Hazelle A. Champlin, hostess of the Wren's Nest; and to others. Acknowledgment should also be made to the D. Appleton-Century Company for permission to lean heavily on Mr. Harris's book, *On the Plantation,* in depicting his boyhood.

Special mention must be made that quotations from three letters by Joel Chandler Harris are made by permission of and special arrangement with Houghton Mifflin Company, authorized publishers.